SOCIAL THEORY
AT A CROSSROADS

Duquesne Studies—Philosophical Series

Volume Thirty-Six

ANDRÉ SCHUWER AND JOHN SALLIS, *editors*

Social Theory at a Crossroads

WILLIAM LEON MCBRIDE

DUQUESNE UNIVERSITY PRESS
PITTSBURGH

Certain portions of chapter two are being published in an essay entitled "Sartre and Marxism," in *The Philosophy of Jean-Paul Sartre*, edited
by Paul Arthur Schilpp (La Salle, Ill.: Open Court Publishing Company, 1980), © 1980 by The Library of Living Philosophers, and are
reprinted by permission of the publisher. A major portion of chapter
four originally appeared as "The Philosophy Job Crisis and the Future of Our Culture" in *The Philosophical Forum*, winter 1978–79, reprinted by permission of the editor, Marx Wartofsky.

First Edition

Library of Congress Cataloging in Publication Data

McBride, William Leon, 1938-
  Social theory at a crossroads.

  (Duquesne studies: Philosophical series; v. 36)
  "A revised version of a series of four lectures . . .
presented at Duquesne University in November 1977."
  Bibliography: p.
  Includes index.
  CONTENTS: The state of social theory today.—Sartre's
contribution to social theory.—Injustices and wrongs.—
Socio-economic bases of the current crisis in our culture.
  1. Social sciences—Philosophy—Addresses, essays,
lectures. I. Title. II. Series.
H35.M16   300'.1   79-25819
ISBN 0-391-01632-6

ISBN 0-391-01633-4 pbk.

To
CATHERINE *and* KARA

CONTENTS

Preface

This book is a revised version of a series of four lectures that I presented at Duquesne University in November 1977. Both in its arrangement of topics and in its critical orientations it was and remains more a reflection of my own assessment of the situation of contemporary social and political theory than an attempt faithfully to reproduce some assumed consensus about that situation. Consequently, it is intended as an original theoretical work, despite the fact that most of its pages are devoted to discussing the writings of others.

At the same time, however, I also designed the lectures, and hence have now designed this book, with a view to providing a basic introduction to its subject matter for an audience assumed to be intellectually sophisticated but not universally well informed about social and political thought. Indeed, the lecture series was taken as a "mini-course" by several students. It was the first of three such series given during the 1977–78 academic year, and I kept in mind the desirability, among other things, of laying a foundation that could be built upon by the two subsequent speakers, my friends Professors Dick Howard, of the State University of New York at Stony Brook, and Richard Bernstein, of Haverford College. I hope that this brief account of the book's genesis will serve to strengthen my claim as to its general and introductory nature, without negating its putative originality.

I wish to thank all the members of the Duquesne philosophy department for their parts in encouraging this enterprise. In particular, I wish to acknowledge my special debts to Professor John Scanlon, who chaired the 1977–78 lecture committee and corresponded extensively with me about the whole project; to Professor André Schuwer, chairman of the Duquesne philosophy department at that time; and to Professor John Sallis, its current chairman, who invited me to make the revisions and additions needed to effect the transformation from lectures to book.

CHAPTER ONE

The State of Social Theory Today
An Overview

Although it has been cited innumerable times when the topic of social and political theory is discussed, there is a passage in Plato's *Republic* that remains, to my way of thinking, the best expression of the basic tension that underlies this entire vast area of thought. Socrates has just launched into a passionate defense of true philosophy, which is said to be a rarity in comparison with the activities of the Sophists; he makes the following observation:

> Each of the private wage earners whom these men call sophists and believe to be their rivals in art, educates in nothing other than these convictions of the many, which they opine when they are gathered together, and he calls this wisdom. It is just like the case of a man who learns by heart the angers and desires of a great, strong beast he is rearing, how it should be approached and how taken hold of, when—and as a result of what—it becomes most difficult or most gentle, and, particularly, under what conditions it is accustomed to utter its several sounds, and, in turn, what sort of sounds uttered by another make it tame and angry. When he has learned all this from associating and spending time with the beast, he calls it wisdom and, organizing it as an art, turns to teaching. Knowing nothing in truth about which of these convictions and desires is noble, or base, or good, or evil, or just, or unjust, he applies all these names following the great animal's opinions—calling what delights it good and what vexes it bad. [117]

I am among those who regard Plato's sarcastic analogy as being directly applicable to much of what passes for theory in the social sciences and, to a lesser extent, in social philosophy today. Furthermore, I concur with Plato in believing that such an

1

approach to social theory is, to say the least, inadequate for providing a satisfactory explanation of social life and, to be less gentle about it, a fraud and a sham.

And yet, if one looks at the matter dispassionately, is such a reaction really justifiable for someone in my position? The very passage that I have quoted reeks of platonic presuppositions, which I also take to be untenable. For instance, there is Plato's stress on the *mercenary* nature of the Sophists: they insist on being paid for imparting their knowledge, or pseudoknowledge if one prefers, to others. But if one is not, as Plato was, born into aristocratic wealth, then what choice has one but to earn wages? And the Sophists did, after all, perform a certain kind of service for their clients: even in Plato's own biased account, the Sophists taught others the workings of the beast in such a way as to enable inherently weaker arguments to triumph over stronger ones in the courts of law and hence to permit those trained by successful Sophists to win lucrative judgments. If the Sophists' teaching was not, in this account, *productive* labor,* it could at least be said to have been sanctioned and encouraged by the economic, political, and legal institutions of Athens and other large city-states of the time, and hence to have provided a socially acceptable way for an otherwise indigent Sophist to earn his means of subsistence.

Furthermore—and here we come to the heart of the philosophical issues that are at stake—Plato's dismissal of the Sophists' practice, as he had depicted it in this passage, really depends on one's accepting some version of the metaphysical system known as the Theory of Forms—the idea, roughly speaking, that the essences of such qualities as the noble and the just and the good itself really exist in all purity in a conceptual space independent of the comings and goings of the actual empirical world; that these essences are knowable, at least in large measure, through a process of insight; and that they can in theory be realized, though in practice never in their perfection, in the institutions of this world. This is especially clear

---

*The question of how to draw the distinction between productive labor and unproductive activity is a fascinating one, particularly in light of Adam Smith's conflicting formulations of the distinction (whereby "productivity" is sometimes equated with the making of material objects, but more centrally with profit-making activity) and of Marx's simultaneous adoption and critique of Smith's more central formulation. See]76] and chapter four of the present book.

from the last portion of Socrates' diatribe about the strong beast and its trainer, which I omitted before and will now cite:

> He has no other argument about them but calls the necessary just and noble, neither having seen nor being able to show someone else how much the nature of the necessary and the good really differ. [117]

But it is my considered judgment that there is no satisfactory evidence that the supremely real world of the Forms of Plato's dreams really exists. In fact I believe that the hypothesis that such a world does exist is an *obstacle* to understanding the ways in which such concepts as "nobility" and "justice" have functioned in different social formations at different times and in different places.

Finally, many scholars of the classics have come to see—although complete clarity on this point is impossible by virtue of the relative dearth of documents—the extent to which Plato's apparently disinterested attack on sophistry, of which the passage that I have cited is of course but one small example, is in fact highly colored by certain broadly ideological requirements to which he was bound. We know, for example, that the martyred Socrates had been popularly regarded as another, though perhaps more than averagely eccentric, Sophist, and that factions in Athens still held him partly responsible for Athens's decline and military defeat—at least they saw him as having been a salient symptom of the decline of the old moral values, if not more directly responsible by virtue of his tutorial involvement with the brilliant and treacherous Alcibiades. Plato was determined to draw the sharpest possible line between Socrates and the other Sophists and to depict his former teacher as the defender of a glorified and purified version of the solid old virtues and of a hierarchical social structure that presumably should accompany them. Plato may very well have been so eager to do this that he was willing to distort quite drastically his portrait of Socrates to serve his own purposes. If even half of these innuendos have some basis in fact, however, as I am sure they do, then I would not like to be a party to any twentieth-century glorification of Plato's political orientation, since such glorification could easily be utilized in support of currently existing social hierarchies that I find extremely destructive.

3

So I have posed a personal dilemma. Whenever I read that passage, I feel strongly that it has the ring of contemporary truth, however accurate it may or may not have been concerning the situation of Plato's own time. Yet I have spent very little effort, as yet, in elaborating on its merits, and several paragraphs raising serious, even devastating, objections to it. I have done so in the guise of a personal report, but of course the objections, in one version or another, draw upon attitudes that are common to vast numbers of professional social theorists and indeed ordinary thoughtful people today. Suppose the state or society—whichever entity one chooses to regard as intended by Plato's analogy—*is* a strong beast, then what follows? It is, so to speak, the only beast that we have, and what could be more useful than a science that seeks exact knowledge concerning its behavior? Indeed, in light of the greater awareness that has developed over the past few years concerning the intelligence, the joys and sufferings, the needs, and, when expressed in ethical language, what have come to be called the *rights* of animals, then the pejorative sting is removed from the very foundation of Plato's analogy. One may, if one wishes, devote one's time to imagining a radically different sort of beast—laid up, to use one of Plato's most famous phrases from the *Republic*, in heaven, and no doubt transformed, in ethereal neo-Platonic fashion, into an angel—but such imaginings can hardly be expected to be accorded grant support, not even from the National Endowment for the Arts. All of common sense seems to militate in favor of encouraging research into actual social and political behavior, especially in view of the growth of new data-gathering techniques that enable us to learn more and more about it.

What is social theory? What is *any* kind of theory? A brief answer, to which I subscribe (though with qualifications that will become apparent in the course of this book), is that a theory in its widest sense encompasses all the elements—methodological, descriptive, and normative—that are combined in one way or another to add to anyone's understanding of a given subjectmatter. That is the meaning of explanation, and of course it allows for the possibility of wrongheaded, misdirected theories. Now, it seems to me that this way of construing the meaning and function of theoretical explanation, if it is accepted, renders untenable the notion that such explanation is

4

radically different in kind from *description*, since description, when it is fruitful for an augmented understanding, is taken to be one of the principal elements of theory. But if this is so, then I cannot consistently charge the data gatherers who dominate the fields of the social sciences today with failing to contribute to social theory. What I *can* say is that they, or at least many of them, have failed to remember, or in some cases have never sufficiently reflected on, the fact that theory also includes (whether in a more or in a less self-conscious form) those other two elements that I have labeled "methodological" and "normative," and that neither one of these elements is unproblematic or given by the very nature of the subject matter.

One very helpful way of looking back on overall trends in social theory over the past half century or more is to regard the social sciences as having developed by increasingly stressing the importance and range of descriptions, even very minute descriptions, of social phenomena, while the relatively tiny group of individuals who could be considered social *philosophers* became more and more defensive in response to the charge that they were not professionally qualified to deal with social descriptions and hence ought to confine themselves to normative issues alone. This became a particularly painful restriction during what was called the heyday of Weldonism, [135] after the late and brilliant social philosopher T.D. Weldon, when a large number of philosophers within the Anglo-American analytic tradition came to be convinced, or at least half persuaded, that the conflicts between pairs of seemingly contradictory propositions containing normative terms were really nonrational, hence strictly inarguable, at base. For some years now, however, countertrends have begun to develop: Social scientists have become more conscious of the fact that phenomena do not automatically offer up to the researcher the methodologies with which they can best be treated, and hence that the concept of methodology is eminently problematic, while most philosophers refuse, whether rationally or nonrationally, to hold to emotivist or noncognitivist theories about normative terms. What all this entails is some confusion, together with the real *possibility* of intellectual ferment, but not necessarily a permanent revival of widespread interest in social theory. For it would be quite possible for the majority of social scientists to concentrate more wholeheartedly than ever on data collecting, to accept certain methodological procedures as canonical for certain purposes, and simply to refuse to engage in any philosophical questioning of presuppositions. And it would be quite possible for the majority of philosophers to turn their backs on the messy world of society and politics, with all its empirical inputs, and to concentrate on constructing possible worlds out of even more complex logical symbols. There exist strong, conformist social and political pressures, in many parts of the world, in these very directions.

It is with this very general, impressionistic picture in mind that I have given the title *Social Theory at a Crossroads* to this book. If there is great ferment in social theory today, there is also a strong chance of everything's going flat. In the remainder of this chapter, I intend to try to pinpoint the areas in which I see some of the greatest ferment and some of the greatest difficulties. In the next two chapters, I shall deal in some depth with two very different philosophical approaches in contemporary social theory that I would like to regard as complementary and that, each in its own way, seem to me to represent an encouraging new direction. In the fourth and final chapter, I shall attempt to deal directly with what will have been alluded to more obliquely in the preceding chapters, namely, the dominant social and economic realities of our time that can be seen to explain, in general terms, not only the current situation of social and political theory, but also a more pervasive crisis in our culture, of which the crisis in theory is a reflection.

Let us turn, now, to my overview. Like any overview, it is going to be biased, adopting a certain perspective: one cannot survey an entire landscape at a single instant. And, again like any overview, it is bound to miss many details, and very likely some important details. In any event, I shall begin by discussing the state of social theory in the social sciences, especially in political science and, to a very slight degree, sociology. I shall then move on to the area in which I am most at home, namely, social and political philosophy, not only because it happens to be my professional discipline, but also because I think that it is in philosophy, if anywhere, that we are most likely to see innovative breakthroughs in social and political theory today.

This is so, not because philosophers are intrinsically more intelligent than other sorts of thinkers, or anything of that kind, but rather because the way in which disciplines are structured in academic institutions today, especially in the United States, works against the encouragement of genuine innovations in theory in the social sciences.

In the social sciences in general, and in political science in particular, a clue to the current state of the art is to be found in the fact that a number of writers and even of academic departments accept the distinction between two different *types* of theory: what is called empirical theory, and what is called normative theory. I believe that this distinction is difficult, or even impossible, to draw in a clear-cut way in theory—if one will excuse the expression—but it is evident to me just how, at least in the political-science profession, it works out in practice. I am now going to be offering a caricature, but I do not think it is a very broad one, at least as it is applied to the political-science department at Yale, with which I had close contact for a number of years, and which has furnished several national officers to the American Political Science Association. The caricature is this: The empirical political theorists are that small but admirable band of generally superior minds within the profession who interpret what the majority of their colleagues actually *do*; such individuals must be watched, however, lest they themselves stray too far from the facts or spend too much time away from the really serious business of data gathering. The normative theorists, on the other hand, are an even smaller band of irrelevant and often unintelligible individuals who seldom obtain grant money and who would be better off among the philosophers, if the latter would have them, if it were not for the fact that graduate students in political science probably ought to be given some background in the classics of Western politics, and these people can provide that. Of course, there are many individual political-science departments that fail to fit this caricature, and academic fashions of this sort are constantly changing, but in my experience it is still uncomfortably close to the truth about the mainstream of a profession in which that word, *mainstream*, seems to be very prominent.

It would be useful to step back a little bit and consider the historical genesis of this situation. American political science assumed a definite shape of its own, as something distinct from the history of political thought, by gradually coming to conceive as its primary mission the study of political behavior—the "angers and desires of [the] great, strong beast" of which Plato spoke. There were a number of landmark writings in this process: perhaps the first was Arthur F. Bentley's *The Process of Government* [18], published in 1908 and, as its title suggests, strongly influenced in its overall conception of the political world by the philosophical thought of John Dewey, and Harold Lasswell's very short book, *Politics: Who Gets What, When, How*, published in 1936 [66], is another that I like to single out because of the unusually close conformity that exists between its title and its contents. Of course, the so-called behavioral movement in American political science was fed by many different intellectual streams, of which John Watson's *psychological* behaviorism was in fact not among the most prominent. I have mentioned the common ground between Bentley and John Dewey, for instance; in the case of Harold Lasswell, at the time of publication of his *Politics* book, the single dominant intellectual influence was a neo-Freudianism that pointed in the direction of regarding practicing politicians as suspicious mental cases. And I am sure that other and sometimes conflicting influences could be isolated and identified, as well—for instance, the grass-roots tradition of American populism and the opposing theories of the circulation of elites, which are traceable to the Italian theorists Vilfredo Pareto and Gaetano Mosca. But we must not become immersed in details here; we are attempting, after all, to gain an overview.

By the time World War II began, the behavioral movement in American political science had started to gain the upper hand within the profession. Immediately after the war, its gains began to be consolidated. One of the most interesting ideological linkages between the new movement and other currents of thought—one of the very few, in fact, that recalled a tradition from before the twentieth century— was James Burnham's book *The Machiavellians: Defenders of Freedom* [23]. Its thesis is, roughly, that Machiavelli's *Prince* constituted a historical demarcation of the first order, one that distinguished the bad, old normative theories, which tended to lead, in practice, to totalitarian political regimes that insisted upon conformity, from the good, new *scientific* study of politics, which points toward openness in social and political practice. I cannot refrain from citing the passage in book fifteen of *The Prince* that is usually taken as pivotal in the development of this new attitude, because it is really so moving and, for those who believe or are even tempted to believe in the existence of an eternal and unchanging set of political values, so very evil:

> It remains now to be seen what style and principles a prince ought to adopt in dealing with his subjects and friends. I know the subject has been treated frequently before, and I'm afraid people will think me rash for trying to do so again, especially since I intend to differ in this discussion from what others have said. But since I intend to write something useful to an understanding reader, it seemed better to go after the real truth of the matter than to repeat what people have imagined. A great many men have imagined states and princedoms such as nobody ever saw or knew in the real world, for there's such a difference between the way we really live and the way we ought to live that the man who neglects the real to study the ideal will learn how to accomplish his ruin, not his salvation. Any man who tries to be good all the time is bound to come to ruin among the great number who are not good. Hence a prince who wants to keep his post must learn how not to be good, and use that knowledge, or refrain from using it, as necessity requires. [89]

As for the implications of this passage in light of the overall context of Machiavelli's writings, however, I think that Burnham very much missed the mark. Antonio Gramsci, writing almost two decades earlier in one of Mussolini's prisons, was far closer to it when he identified his beloved Italian Communist Party as the modern prince [46], but he, too, can be faulted for having distorted the historical record in the interests of a certain cultural and political bias. The study of recent Machiavelli interpretations would make for a very interesting approach to contemporary political theory, but unfortunately it would take us too far afield.

Burnham, it is perhaps worth noting, later became a regular contributor to the right-wing magazine *National Review*. The only conclusion that I would urge readers to draw from this fact is that American political scientists during the post–World War II era were not as much removed from popular political debate as the ideology of the developing mainstream in the profession would have had us believe. That ideology, of course, proclaimed that the ideal social scientist was one who was *value-neutral*—free from personal or partisan bias in his or her pursuit of the political facts, even when those facts themselves were value-laden—when, for instance, what was at issue were attempts to identify the shared political beliefs of certain groups and subgroups. Now this claim certainly did not imply that the majority of social scientists, or specifically of political scientists, always measured up to the stated ideal, nor did it mean that such scientists were not entitled to hold their own beliefs when they were off duty, so to speak. But it is important to recall how tremendously important the ideal of value neutrality (*Wertfreiheit*) was, and still is in many circles up to the present time, in shaping the image of American political science and sociology over the last thirty years or more. It is important, even though for some it has now become a wearisome and outmoded issue, just because it has been so pervasive. Not very many years ago, the very discipline itself was still generally known as "government"—and that name persists in a few academic departments here and there. But "political science" became the popular substitute just because it did correspond more closely with the new dominant ideology within the profession. At the same time, of course, not incidentally, the change brought many added benefits; if one were a member of Congress, for instance, supposedly at the seat of American government, would one not feel more comfortable and safer voting for funds for college departments dedicated to *political science* rather than to the study of *government?*

There is a further reason for reminding ourselves just how strong the bias in favor of value-free social science was, and even today remains, within the mainstream of American political science: It is the fact that, to an impartial observer using some of the very statistical and content-analysis methods that are so dear to this science itself, the output of these years of academic productivity within the discipline appears so frequently and heavily skewed in the direction of a certain set of political and social institutions, namely those of American liberal democratic neocapitalism. I am not passing judgment on this fact (for there is no question that it is a fact): I am simply calling attention, once again, to the blatant inconsistency between it and the proclaimed ideal of value neutrality.

Take, for example, three fairly representative classics in recent American political-science literature—David B. Truman's *The Governmental Process* [167], Robert Lane's *Political Ideology* [65], and Robert Dahl's *A Preface to Democratic Theory* [30]. Truman's book, subtitled *Political Interests and Public Opinion*, deals with the governmental process primarily through a study of the phenomenon of interest groups. Just over two pages in the first chapter of a quite long book are devoted to establishing that "political groups abroad" (by which Truman means primarily Great Britain) follow patterns somewhat akin to those American ones that serve otherwise as his *exclusive* models [168]. Germany and Italy are indexed only once in the entire volume; the references to them come from a book by Robert Brady called *Business As a System of Power*, which Truman cites by way of arguing that the author's thesis about the dominance of big business groups in liberal capitalist states is a hasty and excessive generalization, insufficiently supported by data. My point is that anyone studying Truman's book, which has gone through a number of printings and enjoyed considerable prestige, would be hard put to resist the implication that the governmental process as Truman has sketched it—which is in effect a somewhat cynical but still benign and highly laudatory version of the *American* government process of the mid–twentieth century—is to be regarded as the paradigm for serious, hard-nosed political scientists.

Lane's book is not quite the classic that Truman's is, I suppose, but still it carries with it the prestige of its author's position as past president of the American Political Science Association and, I might add, as a very personable individual. What intrigued me about it when it first came into my hands was its title, *Political Ideology*. This suggested, to someone with my training, a serious effort to come to grips with the common phenomenon of mass mystification—the fact that the ideas of ruling classes at a given time and in a given place often turn out to be the ruling ideas—and, in short, to treat the underlying causes of the tendency among large groups of people, both in modern times and throughout history, to hold social and political beliefs that can clearly be seen to have militated against their own best interests. After all, the concept of "ideology" has a very definite history, traceable to its original use as a pejorative epithet by Napoleon, on through its definitive

11

though very sketchy exposition by Marx and Engels, into its various twentieth-century usages, in which the pejorative connotations sometimes tend to be lost. I am not asking, of course, that historical usage dictate our own usage, but simply that a book with serious pretensions on this topic should grapple with some of the fascinating and indeed fundamental questions in social and political theory that are inevitably conjured up by the term "ideology." Unfortunately, Lane's book does little or none of this; instead, it is devoted to a probing of various sets of recent and contemporary attitudes common among American voters—as its subtitle, *Why the American Common Man Believes What He Does*, suggests.

Dahl's *A Preface to Democratic Theory* is, in fact, a serious theoretical work, which makes some good points. It analyzes certain inconsistencies that Dahl has discovered between two American traditions, both democratic—one of which he calls "Madisonian," the other of which goes by the name "populistic." The problem with this book, too, while it is one of the best of its type and period, is that it encompasses a very narrow range of political possibilities that could reasonably be called "democratic." In short, it equates "democratic theory" with some *American* democratic theories and radiates an almost unbounded optimism—which is usual for works of this time and genre—about the capacities for self-adjustment of the political and economic system supported by these theories. Some years later, in 1970, Dahl published another, shorter book called *After the Revolution?* [28]. This was prompted by the protest movements of the late 1960s and is an effort to make some concessions to those who protested while it denigrates the notion of direct or participatory democracy in favor of the old interest-group pluralism, now somewhat revised and updated. Dahl is willing to see certain socialist measures adopted to reform American society. But in the end he remains tied to the framework of liberal democratic assumptions about the nature of human beings and of society within which the dominant part of modern American political science has remained.

A question that may by now have become obvious to ask concerning my own review here is the following: I am criticizing recent American political science for, among other things, a certain extreme provincialism; but am I not guilty of the same attitude by virtue of the emphasis that I have placed on *Ameri-*

can writers? My defense against this charge is twofold: First, and more weakly, the American milieu is the one in which we are now living as people with an academic orientation, and it is therefore profoundly important that we first achieve a critical understanding of mainstream American political science if we are to discuss contemporary social and political theory and the crisis therein in general; secondly, and more crucially, the most salient single fact about the evolution of the social sciences in Western Europe and indeed throughout the better part of the entire world during the 1950s, the 1960s, and *perhaps* (but here I'm no longer so very sure) the 1970s has been the American hegemony—the extent to which American research, because of its quantity and sophistication and the real political and economic power of the country that has supported it, has served as a temptation, a fad, and often enough a model. I shall document this point when I make my brief nod in the direction of sociology.

A few comments are now in order concerning the small band of normativists within the American political-science profession. I think it a fair generalization to say that this group has been dominated, for many years, by the towering figure of the late Leo Strauss. Now, Strauss's former pupils cannot be said to be a monolithic group either in their political learnings or in their particular areas of specialization. On the whole, however, Strauss's own ideas, as exposited in his *What Is Political Philosophy?* [164], in his polemic with Alexandre Kojève over the reading of Xenophon's essay *On Tyranny* [163], and in his numerous other writings, have exerted a very strong influence over a great many of those who have received their graduate training either from him directly or from one of his close followers. Strauss insisted on a standard of precision and scholarship that is thoroughly admirable. Inspired by his familiarity with premodern Arabic, Jewish, and Christian traditions of secret or esoteric writing—whereby the author's real, often unorthodox message could be revealed to the circle of the initiates and concealed under an apparently orthodox veneer from the masses and particularly from would-be censors—Strauss was able to discover hidden depths of meaning in the classical writers to whom he devoted his own scholarly studies, such as Hobbes, Machiavelli, and Locke. His work on Locke [162], for instance, does much to undermine the bland, quasi-Pelagian

13

self-image that the latter endeavored to project, and it raises many doubts about the wisdom of continuing to regard Locke as the patron saint of modern liberal democratic theory. Strauss's followers, who are frequently well versed in one or another of the classical languages, have also produced some outstanding works of political scholarship, such as Allan Bloom's work on Plato's *Republic*.

At the same time, however, Strauss's own conception of politics and political theory was both eccentric and, in my opinion, highly inadequate. He revived the notion of a battle between ancients and moderns in which, as far as he was concerned, the ancients spoke, as it were, with the voice of God. Modern political thought, he maintained more than once, presented a spectacle of degeneration, not only or even primarily of an intellectual sort, but even more of a moral sort. Machiavelli *was*, for Leo Strauss, an evil man, and such figures as Hegel, Marx, and Nietzsche represented still further turnings downward on the path toward a forgetfulness of the very meaning of the political. In the classical writings particularly of Aristotle but also of Plato and others within that broad tradition, as Strauss understood it, political values were taken to exist truly and absolutely, and the object of *true*, classical political science, as distinguished from what passes for such science today, was the quest for truths about the nature of political reality. He anathematized historical relativism in all its forms. It is small wonder that, although Strauss himself had very little indeed to do with ongoing politics, many of his followers have embraced movements of modern conservatism with considerable enthusiasm.

What I and many other readers find most lacking in Strauss is what, for want of a better expression, I might call a sensitivity to epistemological problems. What warrants one's conviction that he or she has insight into the nature of the good, the true, and the beautiful? When Strauss proclaims it as a typical true proposition of classical political science, or philosophy, that "the aim of war is victory" [165], does not the threat of annihilation under which we all live today make it reasonable to reexamine the very *meanings* of those key terms, *war* and *victory*, and to reassess the contemporary value of the Aristotelian virtue of martial courage, in order to see whether that proposition is now as nearly tautologous as it once seemed? Is

14

it really possible in good conscience, two centuries after the appearance of Kant's *Critique of Pure Reason*, to maintain an unapologetic, even unexamined, stance of classical realism? These are the kinds of questions to which Strauss, throughout his writings, generally disdains to address himself; it is a very serious flaw. If one way of describing the inadequacy of much of modern political-science theory is to say that it sometimes becomes all methodological and nothing else (to recall my earlier claim that adequate theory includes normative, descriptive, and methodological components), one way of summarizing Strauss's views is to say that he entirely lacks an explicit methodology. In a way, then, the opposition between Straussianism and mainstream American political science is nearly total.

One very fascinating book, somewhat neglected nowadays, in which this opposition receives full recognition is a collection entitled *Essays on the Scientific Study of Politics*, edited by a colleague of Strauss's at the University of Chicago, Herbert J. Storing. Strauss contributed "An Epilogue" to this book; it is a small masterpiece of barely restrained vitriol, and it concludes with a paragraph that I cannot forbear quoting. It reads as follows:

> Only a great fool would call the new political science diabolic; it has no attributes peculiar to fallen angels. It is not even Machiavellian, for Machiavelli's teaching was graceful, subtle, and colorful. Nor is it Neronian. Nevertheless one may say of it that it fiddles while Rome burns. It is excused by two facts: it does not know that it fiddles, and it does not know that Rome burns. [161]

The historical problem about all this, I wish to point out in summary, is that for many mainstream political scientists in at least a few of our educational institutions, the complex of orientations and approaches to the field that is loosely termed "Straussianism" represented almost all that seemed to be alive in the field of "normative political theory," or indeed of "political philosophy" as a whole. Even though Straussianism was backward-looking, oriented toward classical thought, it offered a polemical, critical message concerning both contemporary political theory and contemporary political life. But almost no alternatives appeared within the field. There were, of course, some exceptions here and there. I might mention, without attempting to go into details, the contributions of Sheldon Wolin [177], Michael Walzer [170, 171], Hannah Pitkin [115, 116], and the late Hannah Arendt [6, 7], who, although technically a philosopher by employment, seems to have been known to many political scientists. I should also mention two political scientists teaching in Canada (the latter is actually a Scandinavian) who fall outside both the behavioral mainstream and the Straussian countercurrent: C.B. Macpherson [90] and Christian Bay [16]. I must surely have missed many others of equal or perhaps greater importance. But it does not matter, for present purposes, because I have been concerned primarily with delineating the political-science profession's recent self-image, as I have perceived it.

I intend to devote very little space to discussing the recent and current state of sociology. I have several reasons for this. First and most important, I cannot claim to have the degree of familiarity with sociology that I have with political science. Secondly, there seems to me to be a greater gap between American and Continental European sociology than between the political-science pursuits in the two regions; Continental sociology is generally much closer to philosophy, for instance, than American sociology is. Thirdly, it is my perception, from perusing recent professional sociology journals, that sociology is a less clearly defined discipline, in the minds of those who take part in it, than political science is. As Neil Smelser, one of the luminaries in the field of sociology and an associate of the redoubtable Talcott Parsons, writes, in an essay called "The Optimum Scope of Sociology":

> This view of the conceptual scope of sociology yields evidence in favor of a conclusion many of us share—that sociology, by comparison with some other sciences, lacks a single, accepted conceptual frameowrk. The field is diffuse and difficult to distinguish from others because it contains a diversity of frameworks, some of which it shares with other fields such as psychology and social anthropology. If anything, then, sociology is too comprehensive, diffuse, soft in the center, and fuzzy around the edges. These qualities make for a field that is enormously

complex and engaging, but less scientifically adequate than might be optimal. [160]

Fourthly, the recent book *The Restructuring of Social and Political Theory*, by my friend and former teacher and colleague, Richard Bernstein, contains, in its first chapter, "Empirical Theory" [20], an excellent overview of some of the main currents of recent sociology. Bernstein discusses Smelser and Robert Merton, in particular, and shows some of the senses in which their dedication to one or another version of deductive natural science as a model for their fledgling discipline has led to a dead end and a consequent perception of crisis.

Both political science and sociology have appeared to me to open themselves more in recent years than previously to influences from other disciplines, especially philosophy and psychology, and from outside movements. But sociology, because of its vaguer, looser self-definition, has perhaps done so to a greater extent. Radical sociology, which has generally not meant the same thing as Marxist sociology, captured an important place during the 1960s and still exerts a considerable influence. It can hardly be said to have a clear-cut meaning to its practitioners, but some understanding of it can perhaps be gained by going back to the events of May 1968 in Paris, events that came close to overthrowing the French government of the time, and which really began with political activities and a manifesto by the sociology students at the University of Nanterre, the modern, impersonal megaversity in the Paris suburbs. The manifesto was entitled "Why Sociologists?" [27], a parody of a then-recent criticism of recent French philosophy entitled "Why Philosophers?" What the students made clear was that they did not wish to be sucked into the kinds of theoretical practices that characterized what they called "American social science" and to which a couple of their own most distinguished teachers, Michel Crozier and Alain Touraine, had in fact made major contributions. These practices, as the manifesto's analysis showed very well, were designed to reinforce the existing social order in the Western European countries and the United States. They called for sociology to be above all *critical*, rather than above all dedicated to preparing professionals to meet the needs of capitalist enterprise.

The ideological battle within sociology goes on, but often, it seems, without any very deep theoretical roots on either side. Those who have endorsed some version of functionalism have generally felt it incumbent on themselves, as a result of this insurgency, to pay more attention than before to problems of *changes* in social structures, for Parsons and others of the older generation had generally been much more concerned with theoretical accounts of how social systems maintain themselves than with theoretical accounts of how they can undergo fundamental changes. One great source of inspiration in this quest for a model for change has, of course, been the historian and philosopher of science Thomas Kuhn, whose *The Structure of Scientific Revolutions* [64], published in 1962, has come to be placed on more social-science book lists, I dare say, than any other recent book informed by some philosophical perspective. Like so many books that achieve vogues, Kuhn's is distinguished not so much by its extreme carefulness or its being in any sense definitive on anything, as by the fact that it met an intellectual need that was beginning to be felt just at the time. Kuhn himself has admitted the inadequacies, the multiplicity of meanings, of his basic concept of a scientific "paradigm," and yet what is important is not these inadequacies but the service performed by that concept in enabling people in many disciplines to imagine how what may count today as ultra-scientific—and therefore, given the tremendously positive response that talk of "science" evokes, most intellectually respectable and correct—may possibly not count the same way at some time in the future. Of course, this whole notion of changing paradigms is a much more commonplace occurrence in the so-called social sciences than in the natural sciences, which are Kuhn's own special area of interest. This may well be because the whole idea of social science, given the meanings of the word *science* in contemporary English, is a mistake.

If it *is* a mistake, one of the principal reasons for it is the association of *science* with certain narrow conceptions of what constitutes *theory*. To try to sort out these conceptual problems has traditionally been one of the tasks of philosophers, and perhaps it is for this reason that one should not expect either the political-science discipline or that of sociology to generate much really original theory on its own—unless, as happens sometimes, a person with a strong philosophical orientation and training, like a Max Weber, comes to be associated primarily

18

with some other, related discipline. We *should* look to philosophy to take the lead in social and political theory, and I intend
now to examine some of the ways in which recent philosophy
has attempted, with varying degrees of success, to do so.

In philosophy, too, I propose to approach an overview of
social and political theory today from the perspective of recent
history. In the domain of philosophy—more, I believe, than in
that of the social sciences—we are confronted with a great di-
vergence between developments in Continental Europe, on the
one hand, and, on the other, developments in the Anglo-Saxon
countries, meaning primarily Great Britain and the United
States. I shall begin with the latter set of developments, stop-
ping at a point that will be resumed in my third chapter, and
shall then conclude this first chapter by surveying recent social
and political theory in the Continental tradition.

The name T. D. Weldon is not a household or classroom
word even among most philosophers today, but it is of great
importance in understanding political and social philosophy in
the Anglo-Saxon countries during the post–World War II period. Weldon had made a name for himself as a Kant scholar,
and during the war, as I understand it, he had had some re-
sponsibility for decisions about bombings for the Royal Air
Force. In any event, he emerged from his wartime experience
apparently quite shaken in spirit; although I do not subscribe
to the view that personal experiences are alone determinative
of one's philosophical orientation, I do believe them to have an
important effect on the thought systems of at least some, Weldon among them. In 1953 he produced what I consider to be
his most important work, though it has now been out of print
for some time, entitled *The Vocabulary of Politics* [172]. Essentially, it is a landmark in the relatively short-lived movement
known as ethical noncognitivism, and it is of unique importance, within that movement, for political thought. A. J. Ayer,
in *Language, Truth, and Logic* [13], had already made the sweep-
ing claim that terms of moral approval or disapproval had no
more cognitive significance than words such as "Hooray!" or
"Boo!," but Weldon broke new ground by employing his considerable knowledge of the classical works of political philosophy in order to attempt to demonstrate something close to

Ayer's thesis in this specific area. Weldon, to be accurate, was not entirely negative about the contributions made by philosophers such as Plato to political thought; he took these contributions to be the clarification of our political vocabulary, even if clarification was not the principal function that Plato and the others believed themselves to be performing. Weldon did insist, however, that there was no rational basis for choice between any two different and competing "political foundations," as he called alternative world views and sets of principles about politics, such as the one that he designated "democratic" and the one that he designated "Communist." At this level, no genuine argument was possible—at best, perhaps, only personal testimonials about personal attitudes by those who were committed to one or another "foundation."

The atmosphere generated by what came to be known as Weldonism was one of deep despair about the very future of political philosophy. The broader intellectual context, of course, was the rise to dominance of logical positivism, in its various versions, and of ordinary language philosophy, an alternative to logical positivism that at the time was often perceived as an adjunct to it. Philosophy, it was thought, needed to impose upon itself exceedingly rigorous canons of verifiability if it was to remain respectable in a scientific world. Moreover (I doubt that this is a logical consequence of any version of the principle of verifiability, but it can at least be said that the two attitudes often went together at the time of which I am speaking), it was said that philosophers needed to become clear with themselves about the extremely limited scope of their discipline, which could only be second-order and at a meta-level and must refrain from entering into substantive issues that should properly occupy the "experts" in other disciplines, such as physics, psychology, and political science. These strictures, if rigidly adhered to, apparently left political philosophers with very little to do of what, as Weldon had conceded, most of them had traditionally *thought* that they were doing. A few individuals, such as Weldon's contemporary Margaret Macdonald, could assert that "Philosophic remarks resemble poetic imagery rather than scientific analogy" [88], and yet could go on to teach and write articles in the area of political philosophy, on the assumption that the linguistic analysis of such poetic imagery still had something worthwhile

about it. But such a stance, heroic in the light of political philosophers' old aspirations to say something true about political
things, was not for everyone. It was commonly whispered, in
Oxford common rooms, that political philosophy, like Nietzsche's God, was dead.

Well, not quite. At Oxford itself, for instance, Sir Isaiah Berlin, an extremely captivating and popular lecturer as well as a
brilliant mind, kept the spirit alive from his chair as Chichele
Professor of Political and Social Theory. There were of course
others, too, particularly some younger thinkers who were beginning to emerge and to question the very extreme conclusions of the Weldon era, but Berlin deserves special mention
because he was accorded the privilege of contributing the lead
article to the second volume, published in 1962, of the important series *Philosophy, Politics, and Society;* the article is entitled
"Does Political Theory Still Exist?" [19] (It had actually first
appeared, interestingly enough, in a French journal, *Revue
française de science politique.*) Berlin's answer to his question is,
of course, "Yes," for a variety of conceptual and historical reasons. The editors of the volume, Peter Laslett and W. G. Runciman, in their brief introduction, refer to the Weldonian atmosphere that had dominated the first volume of essays, in 1956,
and to the great resurgence of interest in political theory that
had taken place in the six years that elapsed before the publication of the second volume. Before mentioning one or two of
the theoretical considerations behind this resurgence of interest
among philosophers, I wish to make some reference to the
political climate within which these changes from despair to
cautious optimism about the future of political philosophy took
place.

It is interesting to consider to how great an extent the minority currents in post–World War II Anglo-American
philosophy—those that were not under the sway of Weldonism—were in fact dominated by immigrants to our cultural
sphere. In the United States, Carl Friedrich, of the Harvard
government department, founder of the American Society for
Political and Legal Philosophy and first editor of the very distinguished *Nomos* series, and Hannah Arendt were perhaps the
two most prominent names of the time who fit within my
specifications. Both were refugees from Nazi Germany. In
Great Britain, Isaiah Berlin himself was an immigrant, as was

21

Sir Karl Popper, whose work in the related field of the philosophy of the social sciences also deserves notice and will receive
it below. (The influence of these two individuals and of a number of other immigrant intellectuals on various cultural disciplines in twentieth-century England is well documented in an
excessively polemical but fascinating essay, "Components of
the National Culture," in the book *Student Power* [5].) Whatever
their other virtues or faults—and in every case the former far
outweighed the latter—they can all be said to have been tremendously affected by their brushes with totalitarianism in
practice; both Friedrich and Arendt, for instance, are responsible for books (the former as editor and contributor, the latter as
full author) on that very concept, "totalitarianism" [44, 8]. It is
also important to realize that at least three of the four—the case
of Hannah Arendt is not so clear-cut and would in fact be very
interesting to pursue in some other place—played roles as
what political historians later came to call "Cold Warriors,"
champions of Western Liberal democratic practices and ideas
against the perceived Communist menace on the ideological
level. The same can be said, though I think his influence was
more limited to a narrow academic audience than were the
influences of the others, about Weldon himself; his chapter on
"Communist foundations," for instance, contains some un-
wontedly harsh and unsophisticated sloganeering, attributing a
certain barbarism to those who subscribe to such foundations.
Indeed, since Weldon's familiarity with Marx's own work and
with the rich and complex traditions of Marxist theory seems,
on the evidence, to have been rather superficial, and since the
reality of Stalinism was there for all to read about in the daily
newspapers of the 1940s and early 1950s, it should not really
come as a surprise to discover such material.

Thus, the fate of political philosophy then, as always, is seen
to be closely intertwined with the vicissitudes of daily political
life—even, it seems obvious, in the cases of those thinkers
who pretend to be aloof from the political battles and to be
models of dispassionate scholarship. This is not a novel conclusion, of course, but I think it is one of which we all need
constant reminding.

What, now, can be said about the more purely theoretical
considerations involved in the evolution of the atmosphere—
itself coincident, not surprisingly, with the beginnings of de-

Stalinization in the Soviet Union—that led to the demise of the "death of political philosophy" school of thought, or, as a dialectician might put it, to the negation of the negation? There are many ways of approaching this historical question, since there was no single book or article that changed an entire climate in two countries overnight, but I like to focus on one frequently cited passage in T. D. Weldon's book. It goes like this:

> To ask "Why should I obey the laws of England?" is the same sort of pointless question as "Why should I obey the laws of cricket?." It looks rather different because "law" has had a number of different uses and has a lot of religious and semi-mystical ingredients. [173]

That statement was too much for a number of readers to take. It epitomized a certain attitude of extreme insularity that might have had some semblance of reasonableness in the relatively tranquil Oxfordshire countryside at that time, perhaps as one was taking a twilight stroll across Christchurch Meadow, but that made little sense in most polities throughout the world. A series of essays, inspired at least in part by a general reaction against this quintessential declaration of Weldonism, was devoted to the issue of "Why obey?" and whom to obey—the so-called problem of political obligation. Such related notions as authority and legitimacy came to be widely discussed once again by philosophers, and political philosophy began once more to be respectable. Of course, I am overgeneralizing about what was in fact a very slow and complex process.

An important book in this time of renewal, published in 1958, was Peter Winch's *The Idea of a Social Science and Its Relation to Philosophy* [175]. I shall not enter here into details about its contents; once again, I refer to Richard Bernstein's *The Restructuring of Social and Political Theory*, which contains a section on the book [21]. The book has a great many difficulties; it is not even very well organized. I shall simply list, very schematically, a few of the trends that it helped to accelerate.

First, Winch's book broke very firmly with the Weldonian idea that a work in political philosophy should be, as Weldon once put it, about words and not about things—that is, it broke with the notion of philosophy as a discipline that should remain strictly on a meta-level of discourse. Winch traced one branch of the ancestry of this notion back to a very venerable figure in English political theory and philosophy in general, John Locke, who had spoken of the philosopher as "the underlaborer" in the field of knowledge; Peter Winch was not content to be an underlaborer. Secondly, Winch's *The Idea of a Social Science* raised the intriguing possibility, to my knowledge very little discussed before that, that certain key ideas of Wittgenstein's, notably his conception of "rules," could be of fundamental importance for social and political philosophy and indeed could provide a conduit for resurrecting substantive issues. Winch even *hinted*, in a manner that was quite heretical to the dominant orthodoxy of the day, that *Hegel's* thought might still be worth considering. Thirdly, Winch's approach, which included extensive references to Max Weber as well as to Wittgenstein and others, had the effect of broadening his readers' attention from the narrower and historically more time-limited area known as "political philosophy" or "political theory" to the broader area of social philosophy or social theory. A brief digression on this last point is in order here because it seems to me to be of more than purely terminological interest and to be important for clarifying certain of my own perspectives.

It appears, although I have not done the data collecting that would be needed to prove it, that in recent years there has been an increase in college-catalogue references to courses in "social philosophy," or, more frequently, to "social and political philosophy," compared with courses entitled simply "political philosophy." Why this change, at least as I perceive it to be, in emphasis? In part, it seems clear to me, it is because so many of the issues that concern us theorists today are of the sort that put into question, at least peripherally, the very notion of the state. And yet, both etymologically and in much contemporary literature, the idea of the "political" is almost inescapably bound up with that of the *polis*, the state [80]. Of course, the *polis* of Plato and Aristotle was a very different animal from the modern State that is exalted in Hegel's *Philosophy of Right*. (Cf. [11].) Yet there remained a strong continuity in the philosophical focuses of those who wrote about these two kinds of states. But in order fully to understand the nature of the state, we need to have some conception of a logically possible prepolitical or extrapolitical condition; the social-contract theorists, with their various

24

versions of the state of nature, already saw that clearly enough. What is peculiarly modern is the suspicion that even the most utterly modern of modern states may not have to be and in fact, if we could read the future, may not be the *ne plus ultra* of the social organization of human beings. With Marx, for one, the idea of a truly postpolitical society, a new world order in which the trappings of the modern state could gradually be eliminated, as a future possibility rather than a utopian dream, first comes to be taken very seriously. We now realize that Marx was excessively optimistic in many respects concerning this idea, but at the same time many of us have come to recognize more clearly than before that a concentration on such traditional problems of early modern political theory as the branches of government, the idea of equality, and, of course, the basis of political obligation needs to be supplemented by a new, heightened attention to issues as broad and wide-ranging as the nature of everyday life. And to mark this new emphasis, the old term "political philosophy," with all the connotations that it has accrued over the years, is inadequate. What needs to be stressed, then, is that talk of "political *and* social" philosophy is a new trend that, far from being accidental, has important and, to me, positive ramifications.

Winch's *The Idea of a Social Science* was only one manifestation of a general tendency of its time, a tendency to reassert the possibility that social and political philosophers might, after all, be entitled to say something useful and important about society and politics. Another manifestation of a very different sort was the widely read work of Sir Karl Popper, which I have mentioned and which, although considerably earlier in its inception, may (with respect to the time of its greatest popularity) be identified with this same general period. I am referring particularly to two of his best-known books, *The Open Society and Its Enemies* [118] and *The Poverty of Historicism* [119]. Popper, an advocate of "piecemeal" social engineering, was perhaps more impressed by the damage that he thought some social and political philosophers had caused than by the positive possibilities of social and political theory. He regarded it as not only mistaken but also the root of much social evil to attempt to make general prescriptions about the structures and institutions of any allegedly ideal society. Yet this is precisely what he found Plato, Hegel, and Marx, among others, to have done. Popper's criticisms about Plato's alleged totalitarianism are surely one-sided, though just as surely not entirely beside the mark; John Wild enumerated some of Popper's basic errors concerning Plato in *Plato's Modern Enemies and the Theory of Natural Law* [174]. The concepts of totality and totalization and their relationship to the somewhat vague but very powerful and real idea of totalitarianism have been important topics in contemporary Continental social philosophy; they have been sorted out by Sartre and others with a subtlety that Popper lacked. Moreover, when in *The Poverty of Historicism* Popper dismissed Marx as "historicist" (a label of Popper's own devising, to the definition of which much of that book is devoted), he displayed an extremely superficial comprehension of what Marx was up to. Popper did indeed succeed in refuting the notion that it is possible to devise adequate "covering laws" for all of human history that would be analogous to such physical laws as those of gravity or of thermodynamics, but neither Marx nor even, for that matter, Hegel thought that this was what he was doing. What is interesting is that Popper's work was taken so seriously despite the inadequacy of his historical scholarship, no doubt because of the crispness of his conceptual skills.

It is interesting to observe that some of the same kinds of superficial criticism, directed against the mainstream tradition of nineteenth-century German philosophy and its twentieth-century heirs, have seemingly been revived within the last several years by the so-called New Philosophers movement in France. I shall return to consider this and similar phenomena when, in my final chapter, I try to confront the question of the current crisis in our culture. Why this déjà vu experience twenty years later and on the other side of the English Channel?

While the post-Weldonian revival of political philosophy was occurring in Great Britain, we may well ask ourselves what was taking place here in the United States. As a matter of fact, I cannot think of any truly outstanding contributions that were made to social and political philosophy by American philosophers from within the Anglo-Saxon mainstream of postwar philosophy during the fifties and early sixties. I think it fair to say that this period was characterized by a reverence for Oxbridge, which has since faded somewhat, that perhaps made it difficult for Americans within this tradition to generate original contribu-

26

tions. It is not that American contributions had never been made in the past; one need only think, for instance, of John Dewey or of an individual whose work has lately been experiencing a considerable revival, so I am told, among sociologists, namely, George Herbert Mead. But the period to which I am referring was, if anything, even less fruitful within American philosophy, if we exclude figures who departed from the then-fashionable orthodoxy, such as Arendt or Marcuse, than it was within British philosophy. On the other hand, Americans were steady and important contributors to the field of ethics, and this meant that they were familiar with certain conceptions that were of great political and social importance, such as, most notably, the justification of actions, practices, and institutions in accordance with the principles of utilitarianism.

Within the mainstream Anglo-Saxon philosophical tradition on which I have been concentrating this situation of comparative British dominance and American obscurity has been reversed in the more recent past. Whatever criticisms one can make concerning the authors to whom I am about to refer, the climate of discussion generated by their writings and those of many of their colleagues—our present climate of discussion—is very different from the atmosphere of the Weldon period. Almost everyone agreed, when it was published some seven or eight years ago, that John Rawls's *A Theory of Justice* [124] should be taken as a landmark work in this mainstream tradition; it still is taken this way by many individuals. A bit more recently, Robert Nozick's *Anarchy, State, and Utopia* [109] was published, and it, too, has been treated in many quarters as a major effort. Nozick's picture appeared in *Newsweek* magazine [179], and I suspect that he is one of the few philosophers to have been so honored recently, with the exception of the New Philosophers from France and perhaps Sartre and/or de Beauvoir. Even more recently than Nozick, Ronald Dworkin graced *Time* magazine [17], as a result of his new contribution, *Taking Rights Seriously* [38]; he was photographed while boating, fashionably, off Martha's Vineyard. There is, then, somewhat more concurrence than usual between the popular press and the professional philosophical journals as to what counts as "in" these days in social and political philosophy. I shall undertake a slightly more detailed consideration of these works, with special emphasis on Rawls's book, in my third chapter.

The present chapter, after all, is meant to provide only an overview, a survey. Nevertheless, I would like to conclude this part of my survey by offering the following, admittedly tendentious but I believe still essentially accurate, *mise en place* of the three books that I have just named.

Rawls's work is a magnum opus, about a decade in preparation, which aspires to the sort of magisterial definitiveness that we associate (and he himself associates) with the products of periods of greater personal and intellectual luxury than our own, such as Henry Sidgwick's late-Victorian classic, *The Methods of Ethics. A Theory of Justice* is a work of tremendous detail, yet it fails to devote more than a few very brief sections to one of the two major principles Rawls sees as basic to justice, namely, the liberty principle, and, as admitted by its author, it is extremely sketchy on its last major topic, goodness and the relationship of goodness to justice. So it is a modern classic, but a very flawed one in its structure. It attacks the once-dominant current of utilitarianism in contemporary ethical, social, political, and legal theory, and argues that we should carve a new, or perhaps renewed, basis of social thought out of a revived, somewhat more abstract version of the old state-of-nature and social-contract theories. It asserts that there is an ideal of justice to be found, that Rawls has found it, and that we can do so along with him. It does not defend all existing practices and institutions in contemporary American life by any matter of means, but when it comes to discussing institutions that are just it arrives at structures that look remarkably like those provided for by the United States Constitution, though of course with some variations. It reads like a pleasant, though at times slightly tedious, dream. I find it shocking, on the surface, that this book should be a major cultural product of our chaotic, violent late twentieth century, because it is so serene. But it is admirable in its way, and its detailed contentions deserve the sort of respect that one accords a book when one devotes (as I have done) more than half a semester of a course to it.

Dworkin's work, a collection of essays that had been published over a number of years, is perhaps less interesting from the perspective of social and cultural trends. From the standpoint of relevance to current politics, however, Dworkin could hardly have been more successful: he seems to have been prescient in anticipating President Carter's human-rights cam-

28

paign. He is supportive of Rawls on fundamental issues; one of Dworkin's essays [39] expresses this support. This essay, in fact, is more explicit than anything one can find in Rawls's book concerning the essential rightness, from Dworkin's point of view, of the liberal democratic tradition in political theory. Dworkin seems to see himself as the legal conscience of an essentially right-minded polity that has been guilty of some serious mistakes, notable its actions in Vietnam; he is a social commentator and critic, but he is not, like Rawls, a highly systematic theorist.

Nozick's work, by contrast, is absolutely fascinating in terms of the light that it sheds on the present state of our culture; in fact, I am certain that *Anarchy, State, and Utopia* is much more valuable as a cultural artifact than as a philosophical statement about any of the topics that it deals with, with the possible exception of its short excursus into the area of animal rights. It is a self-consciously erratic book; Nozick takes a certain pride in his breeziness of approach and in what might be called the "unfinished look," very much like the vogue in contemporary furniture, that he has succeeded in projecting. Nozick appears as the proud convert to libertarianism of the right—the former participant in late-sixties student demonstrations who now concurs with John Locke, but with a degree of consistency and, one might almost say, of fanaticism of which Locke himself was never capable in viewing property rights, called "entitlements," as the basis of all rights. Nozick approaches the whole range of issues that fall under the heading of "social welfare" with a systematic callousness that contrasts sharply, so I am told, with his considerable personal charm. The fact that his book was published at all in the very unfinished state in which it still exists; the fact that it received a major national book award; the fact that it became a much-discussed topic within the American philosophical community so quickly after its publication; the related fact that the journal *Philosophy & Public Affairs* devoted the better part of an entire issue to excerpts from the book [112] just prior to its publication—these and other such interesting facts can be very easily put together to give us some insights into the mood of social and political philosophy today as it plays itself out within the Anglo-American analytic mainstream. I shall not attempt to dot all the i's and cross all the t's with respect to inferences that could be drawn from the Nozick phenomenon and its significance in relation to the Rawls phenomenon; for the most part I shall simply ask readers to draw their own conclusions, some of which will undoubtedly diverge from mine.

At this point I shall take temporary leave of what I have been calling the "Anglo-American mainstream" in contemporary social and political philosophy. I shall return to it in chapter three. In justification of some of the tendentious remarks that I have just written, I have a plea to make. It is this: There are many, perhaps a majority, of my colleagues who would regard such facts as the personal history of a writer, his or her socioeconomic status, the identity and circumstances of a book's publication, and so on as being possibly of interest to an intellectual historian with a small, picky mind avid for tedious details, but of no philosophical importance whatsoever. A former student of mine, for instance, who has done much of his graduate work at Cambridge University, has told me with enthusiasm of the self-consciously ahistorical approach taken by some of his instructors to the work of Descartes: one reads the Cartesian texts as if they had been written yesterday, deliberately bracketing out all references to the historical Descartes, including the philosophies that he studied as a youth and later rejected while in fact preserving so much from them; the circumstances of his relationship with authorities of the Catholic Church and the French state; and so on. My plea is that such bracketing be disowned as an appropriate way of doing philosophy, unless it is clearly understood in advance that this approach to past and present philosophers is being undertaken strictly as a temporary intellectual game, in the hope that it will uncover some new strength or weakness in them that a less abstract, more rounded and historically oriented approach might miss. The historical details often *are* important, indeed crucial, for understanding just what a philosopher's purpose in writing in the first place was and consequently in determining the very *meaning* of what he or she says. I do not claim that all details are equally important in everyone's case—one must be discerning—but my point is that even a stance of studied *disinvolvement* from issues in social and political theory on the part of a given philosopher may be extremely revealing concerning the nature of the entire philosophy. Indeed, Descartes's "provisional morality" is a marvelous case in point.

30

Let us now shift, abruptly, from the world of mainstream Anglo-American philosophy to that of what is loosely designated the Continental tradition in recent social and political philosophy. To call it this is not, of course, to rule out the possibility of participation in this tradition by philosophers who are British or American; indeed, there has been much participation of this kind. Nor do I want to rule out the possibility of cross-fertilization between the two traditions or perhaps their eventual convergence in one form or another. There has been some such cross-fertilization, although in the last analysis I think one would have to say that there has really been disappointingly little up to the present time. One of my several objects in this short book is, in fact, to add to this cross-fertilization and to *encourage* it. But when I write of the disappointingly small amount that one finds in the recent past, I would like to ask readers of books such as Dworkin's or Rawls's or even Nozick's to consider the references to Continental social and political philosophy to be found in them. One will not find references in any of the three to Sartre, to Merleau-Ponty, to the Frankfurt School, or to the various East European thinkers of note from the past two decades; I have checked this carefully to make absolutely certain of it, though the very thought that some such references might exist seems ludicrous on the surface of it to anyone who is familiar with the nuances of the current atmosphere that I am trying to depict. But is that not sad? In Dworkin's work, which in any case is much less thoroughly referenced than the other two, there is not even a mention of the great Viennese positivist thinker Hans Kelsen, who was such an important intellectual influence on Dworkin's mentor, H. L. A. Hart (Hart himself is of course discussed at length by Dworkin). In Nozick's work, not surprisingly, there are some important references to Karl Marx, at least, though they are extremely polemical and often inaccurate. But once again, as far as references to contemporary Continental philosophers are concerned, there are none, unless one chooses to consider the conservative economist F. A von Hayek a philosopher, and there is a single highly insulting and erroneous reference to Herbert Marcuse [110].

At any rate, the mainstream of recent Continental social and political philosophy, unlike the Anglo-American mainstream, has unquestionably owed its very life and force to the thought

31

of one nineteenth-century individual above all, namely, Karl Marx. I shall document this rather rapidly with a view to raising a critical historical question with which I think we are confronted, to wit: Are we now more or less at or near the close of the era in which this claim of Marx's predominant influence can accurately be made, and, if so, what, if anything, is able or likely to replace it? I ask this because our answer to it will have a considerable effect on how we describe and appraise the current crisis in social and political theory, which is above all a crisis of disorientation and also, to some degree, a crisis of enfeeblement. I also ask this question in light of my beliefs, on which I shall be elaborating in the next two chapters, that (a) Sartre, whose ambivalent relationship to Marxism has always been a matter of great interest to me, offers some very important suggestions concerning the direction that future social and political theory may take and (b) the Anglo-American tradition in it present form, as represented by the three recent writers Rawls, Dworkin, and Nozick, has become mired in certain difficulties of general approach, from which we may in Dworkin's work be able to discern the beginnings of a way out—perhaps with the aid of some ideas and techniques derivable from Continental thought. So much for the outline and the rationale of this final section of the present chapter.

Sartre remarks, near the outset of his essay *Search for a Method* [152], that Marxism remains the dominant philosophy of our epoch. Other philosophical tendencies, he says, represent either reactionary echoes of earlier world views or, alternatively, approaches to certain aspects of reality that are marginal to or parasitic upon the dominant Marxian world view. It is within the parasitic category that he places existentialism, which he regards as having come to grips with problems of the individual at a time when the current of Marxism that considers itself "orthodox"—Marxism-Leninism, if one prefers—had neglected these problems and become temporarily ossified. But he looks forward, or at least he did look forward at the time of the writing of this essay, now some twenty years ago, to an eventual reintegration of Marxism with existentialism. Beyond that, it is important to note, Sartre also speaks of the ultimate supersession of every form of Marxism as a dominant world view by what he calls a "philosophy of freedom," which will become a realistic possibility when scarcity has been overcome.

Nowadays, Sartre has second thoughts about the identification of his own philosophy with the Marxism to which he then subscribed. He believes that the emphasis on freedom that is to be found in his own thought remains its single most salient feature—a point on which most critics could probably agree—and that Marxism is lacking in this feature, which is a more debatable point. But I shall discuss such matters in my next chapter. My reason for introducing Sartre's contentions, made in the mid-1950s, about Marxism's dominance is that they are an important expression of a widespread attitude of Continental theorists of this very recent period; as such, I believe them to be true, even though they are vague and open-ended enough to elude any really rigorous attempt to specify their *exact* significance. Sartre was, in other words, expressing a zeitgeist, a cultural atmosphere, when he made those comments. And there is something important about what he said.

Let us consider some of the best-known Continental thinkers of the post–World War II period, besides Sartre himself. Take, for instance, his close companion, Simone de Beauvoir. In *The Second Sex* [35] and *The Ethics of Ambiguity* [32] she establishes a certain critical distance between her own thought and that of Marxism, particularly the so-called orthodox Marxism, with its stress on historical determinism. It is important for her to establish this distance and not, for example, to reduce the practices of sexism over the centuries to just one more form of class warfare, as some socialist feminists have attempted to do. But it is equally important for her to show that sexism is in very large measure *economic* exploitation and to argue, in her work on ethics, that commitment to historical, political change in the interests of the oppressed and exploited is basic to her notion of authentic existence. On both scores, Marxism or neo-Marxism provides much of the framework for the problems that she considers most crucial. And much of what is not distinctively Marxian in her orientation has historical antecedents, as she herself admits, in the thought of Hegel.

Consider next Albert Camus. His last important philosophical essay was *The Rebel* [25]. This book, as I conceive of it, is above all a repudiation of what might be called "Marxism in practice," the Communist movement, and more generally a repudiation of the activist political life as a snare and a delusion. Camus's subsequent polemic with Sartre [24], occasioned by a review of the book in the magazine that Sartre edited and resulting in a definitive break in their friendship, centered precisely on Sartre's claim that Camus was trying to escape from participating in history and Camus's insinuation that Sartre was in effect excusing such monstrosities as the Soviet slave-labor camps in the name of Marxist, even if not Communist, political commitment.

Or consider Maurice Merleau-Ponty, whose reputation has recently been enjoying, it would seem, a deserved revival. Merleau-Ponty wrote two major works in political and social philosophy, *Humanism and Terror* [106] and *Adventures of the Dialectic* [104]. Both concentrate on problems raised within the twin perspectives of Marxist theory and Communist practice. The later book, *Adventures of the Dialectic*, is decidedly less sympathetic to Communist practice than the earlier one was, and in it Merleau-Ponty pleads for a new political vision beyond those of both Marxism and capitalism—a plea that sounds surprisingly close to what Sartre himself has seemed to be saying more recently. Figures other than Marx, such as Max Weber and György Lukács, also claim Merleau-Ponty's attention in his political writings, but these two and the others stand within the same general tradition.

Many students of Merleau-Ponty's would like to try to separate his political writings from his work in philosophical psychology undertaken from a phenomenological perspective. I do think it fair to say that Merleau-Ponty himself never quite succeeded in satisfactorily joining these two parts of his philosophical output in an explicit, integrated synthesis. But, in the first place, any such synthesis would have been somewhat foreign to the spirit of Merleau-Ponty's thought; moreover, anyone approaching social and political questions from a phenomenological perspective must either eventually confront or else try to disregard the fact that most of the lifework of the founder of modern phenomenology, Edmund Husserl, is highly apolitical. However, I find no evidence that Merleau-Ponty himself regarded his social and political work as an embarrassment or as potentially incompatible with his writings on behavior and perception, and at the same time there are many references within the latter to problems and concepts, such as social class [107], that emanate from a cultural milieu in which Marxism is a dominant force. I therefore find the tendency to dichotomize the thought of Merleau-Ponty between the epistemological and the social and political to be most unfortunate and unwarranted, and I thus consider him as also exemplifying my (and Sartre's) point about the brooding presence of Marx in recent Continental thought.

One of the important intellectual phenomena of the late 1960s and 1970s in France has been a gradual shift of interest, among students of contemporary philosophy, from existentialism and phenomenology to that even more loosely united congeries of approaches that goes under the name of structuralism and that some of those whom we would perhaps like to designate as structuralists wish to repudiate. The interesting aspect of this development for my present purposes is the extent to which Marxism has (at least until the past couple of years, if not still) remained a dominant intellectual tradition even through and across this shift. Claude Lévi-Strauss, the initiator of this movement as much as it is attributable to a single person, claims in one sense to be a Marxist, in that he believes in a kind of material determination of intellectual and cultural structures. Louis Althusser, an extremely important figure in the past decade of French thought, is a Marxist-Leninist "hard-liner" of sorts, who has applied structuralist techniques to the reading of *Capital* and to the general notion of Marxism as a science. And even some of the other leading figures of recent French philosophy, such as Jacques Derrida and Michel Foucault, while they cannot be considered Marxists in any very intellectually rigorous sense, nevertheless show an extremely important formative influence from the Marxian tradition. For instance, Foucault's recent book, *Discipline and Punish* [42], a study of the origins of modern penal institutions, remains heavily dependent on a sense of how what Marx would call the ideological superstructures of society are the outgrowths of socioeconomic conditions.

In short, Marxism has been extremely, nearly totally, dominant in French social and political philosophy over the past three decades; one can discern a few exceptions to this rule, to be sure, but very few. And even these exceptions have often had their intellectual productivity and thought shaped by their felt need to react *against* Marxism, much in the way that Sartre claimed near the opening of his *Search for a Method*. As an illustration of this tendency I might cite Sartre's contemporary and onetime associate, the sociologist Raymond Aron [9].

It is only now that one begins to have a strong sense of a shifting climate. Jean-François Revel, the author of *Without Marx or Jesus* [133], is a popularizer whose work has never attained the degree of philosophical seriousness of a Sartre or a Merleau Ponty or an Aron, but the very popularity of his work attests to the beginnings of this shift. Now the New Philosophers, Bernard-Henri Lévy and André Glucksmann and others, are apparently repeating some of the criticisms that one found twenty-odd years ago in Camus's *Rebel* or Popper's attack on historicism. The key word, I am told, is *contestation*, that is, confrontation with Marx and the Marxist tradition, rather than total disregard of it. But one does sense that French social and political thought is at some sort of a turning point; it is impossible to predict with confidence what will come next.

There are two other geographical areas within the larger whole of Continental thought to which I wish to refer, namely, Germany and Eastern Europe. Recent German philosophy has not been very strong in social and political theory, except perhaps in the more specialized area of legal philosophy, and most of the important works in that area are not translated into English. Ten or fifteen years ago, the imposing figure was Heidegger, and it is almost the case that the less said about Heidegger's political thought, the better. On the other hand, Heidegger's analysis especially of everydayness has led to several interesting attempts to fuse his thought with Marxism. However, the most significant of these attempts have for the most part been undertaken outside Germany. I am thinking of Kostas Axelos in France [12], Karel Kosík in pre-invasion Czechoslovakia [63], and Gajo Petrović in Zagreb, Yugoslavia [114]. Petrović, in fact, is at present working on a book-length Marxian critique of Heidegger's philosophy that I think will be a very important philosophical event when it is completed. Heidegger is known to have acknowledged the tremendous importance of Marxism owing to Marx's concern with historicity, but neither Heidegger nor his closest German followers have, to the best of my knowledge, done much with this assertion in their philosophical writings.

There existed, before the Second World War in Germany, the very famous Frankfurt School, which of course drew strong inspiration in the fields of psychology, sociology, literary criticism, and philosophy from the Marxist tradition. I do not have

36

the space here to delve into the details of that school and its leading figures; there has been a great upsurge of interest in it here in the United States in recent years, and Martin Jay's history of the school [57] furnishes very precise information. I do want to note, however, that it was this school that provided American philosophy with its greatest breath of fresh inspiration from outside the Anglo-American mainstream during the 1960s, in the person of Herbert Marcuse. Marcuse was, like almost all the prewar members of the Frankfurt School, forced into exile by the rise of the Nazi movement; unlike some others, however, he chose to remain in the United States after the war. A few years ago, when one spoke to a group of graduate students with any interest whatever in social and political philosophy, one could take for granted that they knew something about Marcuse's thought and had read at least his *One-Dimensional Man* [94], if not also several other of his works. But intellectual enthusiasms come and go, very largely in response to changing political and social conditions, and it is my experience that one can no longer assume familiarity with Marcuse as a universal phenomenon. Today, I think, it is important to look back upon him as a great synthesizer—of Marx with Freud, of the dialectical tradition from Plato to the twentieth century, of the results of Marxist economic analysis with an imaginative, highly utopian vision of an aesthetic future society. It is important to remember that Marcuse's favorite pages in Marx's work were the sections of the *1844 Manuscripts* in which Marx waxes most eloquent about the possibilities of liberating the functions even of the human senses in a society in which alienation will have been overcome; it is in such passages that philosophy does, indeed, become poetry, just as Margaret Macdonald said it always was.

There is still tremendous interest in Marcuse, as a name and as a congenial and still commanding personage, right up the the time of his death in July 1979. But I think that the content of his philosophical message is in the process of being forgotten, just as it is a little difficult to comprehend that the Marcusean slogan, "Power to the imagination!," was the single most popular watchword during a student revolt in Paris that very nearly succeeded in toppling the French government a decade ago. It all seems very long ago now. I shall try to revive the memory of Marcuse, very briefly, in my final chapter.

37

The so-called New Frankfurt School in Germany, the younger generation, has had what I consider mixed success in recapturing the social and political orientation of the older generation. Jürgen Habermas and Karl-Otto Apel are more or less contemporaries, though Habermas is slightly older and became known earlier. Habermas's inspiration is certainly in part Marxian, for Marx is indeed within the mainstream, as Habermas sees it, of the development of German philosophy, and Habermas shares Marx's opposition to idealism of the Hegelian type. Habermas's institute for social studies in Starnberg, near Munich, has come under serious attack from the right-wing forces that are recapturing control of the West German universities. But there are tendencies in Habermas's thought to move away not only from the Marxism of Marx, which is obvious and which he makes clear [47], but also from a social and economic focus in general to one on philosophy of language and epistemology. The work of Apel, which is now becoming better known, is far less oriented toward social and political issues and far less critical of certain forms of idealism than is Habermas's. In any case, I suspect that, despite Habermas's importance (Richard Bernstein, for instance, regards Habermas as the ultimate development thus far in the restructuring of social and political theory that is the topic and title of his recent book), the present climate in West Germany is not very conducive to a strong, vibrant interest in this area of philosophy. By "climate," I mean not only the intellectual climate defined by such diverse phenomena as the philosophical orientations of Habermas and Apel, the apparent decline of interest in Heidegger, and the growth of interest in language philosophy, but also, and equally important, the development of a political climate of repression and fear resulting from the policy of threatening and in some cases eliminating the jobs of political dissidents, a policy popularly called *Berufsverbot* by its critics. This recent development in German government and university life has not been sufficiently reported on or understood in the United States. When repression achieves a certain degree of severity, then there is by definition no possibility for social and political philosophy to flourish, no matter how great the potential for outstanding contributions there may be within some members of the community in question.

If this truism can perhaps be applied today to West Germany, it is of course applied constantly, and with good reason, to the countries of Eastern Europe, now including Yugoslavia. For there was a time in the late 1950s and the 60s when some of these countries produced remarkable works of social and political philosophy, all of them written, with greater or lesser degrees of orthodoxy, within some kind of general Marxist framework. The work of such writers as Leszek Kolakowski in Poland, Lukács and some of his younger followers (e.g., Agnes Heller and György Markus) in Hungary, Ernst Bloch in East Germany before he decided to settle down for his last years in West Germany, Kosík in Czechoslovakia, and most of all the Yugoslavs was remarkable for its diversity and creativity within that framework. I am very much afraid, however, that the gradual refreezing of thought and culture that was begun in Eastern Europe with the Soviet invasion of Budapest in 1956 and reached its climax in the invasion of Czechoslovakia in 1968 has had the effect of drastically curtailing this whole movement, at least for the time being. (I documented a moment in this unhappy development in my report, "Summer School in Korčula, in 1974 [87].) Some philosophers simply lost interest in Marxist thinking and, frequently along with this, in social and political thought generally. Others, such as Kosík, Markus, and some of the Belgrade philosophers in Yugoslavia, remain repressed and unable to publish freely in their native countries. The Belgrade people are at least still able to publish and travel abroad, and their colleagues in Zagreb and elsewhere are still able to teach and write, but the threat of even worse repression remains. Is it possible to imagine a regrouping of this intellectual tradition in Eastern Europe within the near future? Perhaps. There is a plan to revive the suppressed Yugoslav philosophy journal *Praxis* by publishing it abroad. But the political climate has changed so much that one cannot be too sanguine about the short-term possibilities.

I have crammed a great many names and a great many evaluations, often necessarily superficial, within a few pages. My purpose has been to indicate, as concisely and as honestly as possible, my perception of the state of social and political theory today. True, I have confined my survey to the United States and a handful of other countries. However, there is no question that university professors and intellectuals in many, if not most, other parts of the world look for leadership to the countries upon which I have focused; we know the historical reasons for this. So I am reasonably confident that the overview I have provided has considerable validity with respect to the state of social and political theory throughout the world today, and not just within the countries that I have explicitly mentioned.

I can summarize quickly by saying that there is indeed a crisis. Within the sphere of Continental thought, there are a few disturbing indications that social and political theory may in fact be dead or dying, as it was in England and the United States about twenty five years ago. This is not, of course, to deny the possibility of a future resurrection; in fact, I would rather confidently expect it. Here in the United States, on the other hand, as well as in England, there is a much more positive climate of thought concerning the possibility of social and political theory than there was a generation ago. But some of the major recent products of this climate have been disappointing, a claim that I shall try to validate in more detail in my third chapter. I am convinced that in order to generate a new era of robust social and political philosophical analysis in this country we need to import a great deal more of the spirit and concerns of recent Continental philosophy into our own mainstream. There are university philosophy departments where this is being done, but not nearly enough. Such importation, to be successful, must not be uncritical or adulatory. We can learn from that tradition, and still go on to develop original turns of our own. In the next chapter I shall discuss one figure from whom I think there is an especially great deal to learn, Jean-Paul Sartre.

CHAPTER TWO

Sartre's Contribution to Social Theory
A Retrospective Glance

Hegel, in the preface to his *Philosophy of Right,* makes the following profoundly conservative remark:

> After all, the truth about Right, Ethics, and the state is as old as its public recognition and formulation in the law of the land, in the morality of everyday life, and in religion. What more does this truth require—since the thinking mind is not content to possess it in this ready fashion? It requires to be grasped in thought as well; the content which is already rational in principle must win the *form* of rationality and so appear well-founded to untrammelled thinking. [52]

There is an important sense in which Hegel is quite correct, and an equally important sense in which he is very wrong. I think it may be worthwhile to consider both of these senses, briefly, as a backdrop or introduction to the topic at hand, Sartre's contribution to social theory. I am devoting an entire chapter to Sartre because I think that Sartre has a singularly important contribution to make to social theory today. I believe this even though I know it to be very much of a minority opinion, not only among social and political theorists, but also among those philosophers who regard Sartre's work with great approval.

But what does it mean to have made a "contribution" to this field? By what criteria are we to judge that Sartre has or has not made a particularly salient contribution? That is where Hegel's comments come in. There are a number of reasons for beginning this chapter with the passage from Hegel that I have cited. First of all, I believe that we can never understand a contemporary state of affairs, even one such as that of the present, in which there is a profound intellectual rootlessness and sense of forgetfulness of the past, if, in trying to reflect on

41

that state of affairs, we do not attempt to place it in a historical perspective. So I began with a quotation from Plato in my first chapter, because I thought it was very apt for illuminating the situation of social and political theory particularly in the social sciences today, and so I now recall Hegel. Of all the intellectual influences on the thought of Sartre, even on the more strictly social thought of Sartre, there is none greater than Hegel's. If there is a single earlier classic of philosophy to which Sartre's *Critique of Dialectical Reason*, upon which I shall be focusing here, bears closest resemblance, it is Hegel's *Phenomenology of Mind* though even that comparison is not *very* close. And yet Sartre is, by almost any standards that are commonly employed even by the popular press, a fairly radical thinker, politically speaking. Whereas Hegel, as anyone reading the above quotation would immediately agree, was profoundly conservative—not reactionary, to be sure, but still very conservative.

If one approaches the *Philosophy of Right* for the very first time, without preconceptions, and reads those lines in the preface, one is likely to expect a book in which ancient alleged verities are reaffirmed; in which established morality, law, and religion are upheld and given philosophical justification; in which the *philosophia perennis* that is said to be embodied in the thought of Plato and Aristotle and many later thinkers is restated with appropriate reconciliations and smoothings of the edges; et cetera. In a way, all this *does* happen in the body of Hegel's book. Yet in another way even this *Philosophy of Right*, which is the product of Hegel's later and most conservative years, and hence has often been treated as a disappointing retreat to reaction by modern left-wing Hegelians such as Herbert Marcuse [95], is also a profoundly subversive document. It is subversive, at least, of those very patterns of conservative philosophical and popular thought to which it at the same time pays so much respect, and it is this fact that makes it original, novel— in short, a landmark contribution to the history of social and political theory, one of the greatest classics in our tradition. When, for example, at the end of his treatment of civil society [53], Hegel talks about the tendency within the modern world for the living standard of the masses to fall below a subsistence level; for individuals to lose their self-respect under these conditions; for "the concentration of disproportionate wealth in a few hands" to accelerate at the other end of the social scale; and for this inner dialectic, as he puts it, of modern civil society to drive it to seek markets in backward regions beyond its own borders, then we already have a brief outline of another classic that was to be published nearly fifty years later, Marx's *Capital*. To someone who feels at home with dialectical ways of thinking and with the dialectical rhythms of our world, this paradox about Hegel's contribution to social and political theory—the profoundly conservative mind generating potentially revolutionary thought—comes as no great surprise.

This brief reference to Hegel has been intended only as a backdrop, as I said, to my treatment of Sartre. It would be completely out of character for Sartre, in contrast to Hegel, to claim that the truths he is expounding are simply the rational reformulations of ideas that are as old as the existence of human societies and the first occurrences of productive human labor. Indeed, from his earliest philosophical writings on, Sartre has attempted to *deny* that there is even such a thing as a common human nature *or* a fixed individual character, at least as these notions have typically been used by metaphysicians and philosophers of psychology. (If he is right about this, then it would be impossible for him to write either out of character or *in* character, for that matter!) Nevertheless, despite, or perhaps in keeping with, his espousal of radical political movements in our society, much of Sartre's contribution to social and political thought consists in a certain assimilation of, and response to, currents that were already in place even before he was born—Marxism, Hegelianism, the elusive tradition of Jean-Jacques Rousseau, and others that antedate even those. But to say this is not, in my opinion, to find flaws in Sartre's work in this area; to regard these links with the past as a fatal flaw is to accede to a certain superficial modern conception, the same one that caused Hegel to write what I have quoted back in 1821, to the effect that only what is radically and totally novel is worthwhile. Of course, there can be no such thing; as I have shown elsewhere [74], if we take the idea of radical novelty literally, it disintegrates into nonsense or total madness. Sartre's exploration of this very idea within a social context in his *Critique of Dialectical Reason*—as epitomized in what he calls the "group in fusion" or "fused group" at its moment of "Apocalypse"—actually serves to illustrate this point as it is applied to social practice.

So Sartre's *Critique* is, in part, a work of synthesis of many past ideas; how could it be otherwise if it is really an attempt to tell us the truth about social life? How can we be surprised by the claim that Sartre is attempting to reflect rationally on what was already, in a certain sense, "known," when we call attention to the fact that the concrete event that he takes as most pivotal for purposes of illustrating his abstract analyses is the French Revolution—the very same event, or sequence of events, that was the profoundest historical influence on the young Hegel? Yet Sartre's references to his intellectual ancestors, even to Marx except in a few sections of his book, are quite sparse; he often assumes a certain intellectual culture, which many of his readers do not have.

It is a difficult book—filled with a certain technical jargon that is at times unnecessarily complex, and produced under conditions of extreme tension, when Sartre was ingesting a variety of drugs and would write, as Simone de Beauvoir tells us in her autobiographical work [33], page after page in a white heat, without ever turning back to make editorial corrections. It is also only half a book; what we have is labelled *Volume One, Theory of Practical Ensembles*. Sartre tells us near the beginning and again at the end of this volume (first published in France in 1960) that there will be a second volume, which will place his analyses in a diachronic or historically sequential perspective, as distinguished from the synchronic or ahistorical perspective of the first volume. But volume two has never been written, at least not in any sense in its entirety. We are told [155] that there exist several hundred pages of notes toward a second volume, and perhaps they will be published sometime after Sartre's death, but that is not satisfactory. The principal excuse Sartre has given for not completing volume two is that to do it properly would require him to achieve a level of understanding of non-Western histories—the histories of the *rest* of the world's cultures—that it is too late in life for him to begin to acquire. By now it is certainly too late, since he is invalided and unable to read for himself because of the poor condition of his eyes. And all of these considerations of inadequacy and flawedness also contribute to the feeling, which many critics have expressed, that Sartre's *Critique* cannot be the landmark contribution that he had perhaps hoped it would become.

I must obviously dissent from this evaluation, and I intend

to try to explain why. I shall divide my task, for the remainder of the present chapter, in the following way. First, I shall provide a short historical sketch of Sartre's road to writing the *Critique*, which for him was a road to full social consciousness—by which I mean the consciousness of a social and political theorist, as distinguished from that of a thoughtful man and philosopher concerned about everyday political events and social phenomena. Then I shall summarize the *Critique* very hastily, its main arguments and directions. I shall conclude my historical sketch by quickly referring to Sartre's more recent activities. The second half of this chapter will be devoted to the more strictly philosophical issues for which the first half will, it is hoped, have laid the historical and other groundwork. I shall then deal with a series of problems or questions about what Sartre's contribution to social theory amounts to—its strong points and its weak points, its values and disvalues.

It is appropriate, I think, to speak of this as "a retrospective glance," because, alas, Sartre speaks and is being treated like a person whose career is more or less over. This situation is a function both of his serious illness and of the way in which, as he might express it, he has freely chosen to live this illness and other conditions of his present situation. It is not, as we can attest from other contemporary examples, such as that of the late György Lukács or of the late Ernst Bloch or, nearer to home, of Brand Blanshard or Paul Schilpp, a necessary function of Sartre's having passed the age of seventy.

I shall not assume a detailed prior knowledge of Sartre's career on the part of my readers. Sartre tells us about his childhood in his autobiography, *The Words* [158]. The family environment in which he grew up, for which he now expresses a certain loathing, was a comfortable petty-bourgeois intellectual one, conducive to his coming to believe, as he says he did from an early age, that he would be a writer and that words were more real and more important than things. In this milieu there was no concept whatsoever of a politically and socially committed literature, such as one finds in his 1947 essay *What is Literature?* [157]. As the French equivalent of an American college student, he attended the Ecole Normale Supérieure in Paris, an all-scholarship school for the intellectual elite of future writers and humanists from throughout the country, where of course he developed his interest in philosophy. He made a brilliant record as a graduate student at the Sorbonne, where he became acquainted with de Beauvoir and some of the other close companions of his later life. De Beauvoir's description of the intellectual aspects of Sartre at this time reinforces, in my mind, the picture that I have already tried to present of him as a very close student of the major classical ànd early-modern traditions in the history of Western philosophy. She says [34] that at one point he was especially interested in Rousseau's philosophical work; I think that this should be taken as an important clue in unlocking the secrets of the *Critique of Dialectical Reason,* written so many years later. Sometime after completion of his graduate work he had the opportunity to study for a year at the French cultural center in Berlin, where he absorbed many of the ideas and the phenomenological method of Husserl with the aid of some of Husserl's students. This was the Berlin of the early Nazi period, as depicted in the musical *Cabaret.* During the next decade and more it was the rise of fascism that dominated Sartre's political consciousness; one finds many references to these concerns in his writings and in de Beauvoir's autobiographical material. However, Sartre was at that time unable to do very much by way of assimilating these concerns with his more strictly philosophical essays.

One of these essays, though not the earliest, is "The Transcendence of the Ego." It is intended as a criticism of the turn toward idealism that Sartre sees Husserl as having taken, particularly in his *Cartesian Meditations.* Sartre tries to show that the construct of a transcendental ego, which Husserl developed there, is unnecessary for his purposes and counterproductive to the Husserlian goal of furnishing us with the bases of a presuppositionless phenomenology of the contents of consciousness: this phenomenology had been supposed to be presuppositionless not only with respect to the contents but also and equally with respect to consciousness itself, which Husserl insisted that we always regard as a "consciousness-of." The entire essay provides us with the historical background for understanding the origin of Sartre's full-blown ontology in his great work *Being and Nothingness,* in which being-for-itself, the fount of activity, creativity, and consciousness in the world, is always defined as being, in itself, nothing. What I wish to single out from the essay is a concluding passage in which Sartre is explaining some of the reasons why his alternative theory of the ego as a constructed phenomenon, the product of reflection, is superior to the later Husserlian philosophy. It reads as follows:

> The theorists of the extreme Left have sometimes re-proached phenomenology for being an idealism and for drowning reality in the stream of ideas. But if idealism is the philosophy without evil of Brunschvicg, if it is a phi-losophy in which the effort of spiritual assimilation never meets external resistances, in which suffering, hunger, and war are diluted in a slow process of unification of ideas, nothing is more unjust than to call phenomenolo-gists "idealists." On the contrary, for centuries we have not felt in philosophy so realistic a current. The phenome-nologists have plunged man back into the world; they have given full measure to man's agonies and sufferings, and also to his rebellions. Unfortunately, as long as the *I* remains a structure of absolute consciousness, one will still be able to reproach phenomenology for being an es-capist doctrine, for again pulling a part of a man out of the world and, in that way, turning our attention from the real problems. It seems to us that this reproach no longer has any justification if one makes the *me* an exis-tent, strictly contemporaneous with the world, whose ex-istence has the same essential characteristics as the world. It has always seemed to me that a working hypothesis as fruitful as historical materialism never needed for a foun-dation the absurdity which is metaphysical materialism. In fact, it is not necessary that the object precede the subject in order for spiritual pseudo-objects to vanish and for ethics to find its bases in reality. It is enough that the *me* be contemporaneous with the World. . . . [156]

And finally, a few lines further, he ends his essay with the following words:

> No more is needed in the way of a philosophical founda-tion for an ethics and a politics which are absolutely positive.

There are many things of great interest about this passage for a student of Sartre's thought. First of all, there is the expression of a deep ethical and political motivation for his epistemological and ontological analyses—the principal reason for my citing the passage at length. Then there is the clear-cut expression, so common throughout Sartre's career, of a desire to escape idealism at all costs. There is the claim that no more realistic philosophy than that of phenomenology has come along in many centuries.

Finally, there is the unmistakable Sartrean "put-down" of materialism considered as an ontology or metaphysics (I do not think that the technical distinction between ontology and metaphysics that we find in *Being and Nothingness* is of importance here); and there is, right alongside this denigration of the official doctrine of Marxist-Leninist orthodoxy, the equally unmistakable approval that Sartre is according to historical materialism as what he calls a "working hypothesis."

He was to say much the same thing a few years later in his essay "Materialism and Revolution," in which he remained very anxious to distinguish his position from materialism as an ontological position and hence from what he then took to be Marxist theory; this is the famous essay in which Sartre claims that there is a need to develop a substitute philosophy that can serve the purpose of proletarian revolution as well as the myth of metaphysical materialism has served it, while yet being a true philosophy and not a myth [150]. If we look ahead to his later work, and notably to the *Critique of Dialectical Reason*, we can see that he himself has attempted to develop just that true philosophy that he called for in "Materialism and Revolution" and that he anticipated in a way in the final sentence of "The Transcendence of the Ego," while becoming more and more nuanced in his views about materialism as an ontology. Indeed, at the present time it is no longer incorrect to identify his position as a certain specifiable version of materialism.

But before looking any further ahead, let us go back to the linchpin work of Sartre's career as a philosopher, *Being and Nothingness*. It is a magnum opus; is it his *maximum* opus? In one sense, surely: it made his name as a leading philosopher. In another sense, the quantitative sense, surely not: it is shorter than the *Critique*, and it is dwarfed by *The Family Idiot*. I have always argued [77] for the essential continuity of thought between *Being and Nothingness* and the *Critique*, and Sartre himself has indicated that he is in agreement with this point of view. So perhaps one ought to treat the two *together*, along with *Search for a Method*, the shorter and more popular essay that serves as the preface to the French edition of the *Critique*, as constituting the core of Sartre's lifetime philosophical work.

In any case, political and social questions figure very little indeed in *Being and Nothingness*, though there is an attempt to lay some ontological foundations for a theory of society, of intersubjectivity, in the part of *Being and Nothingness* entitled "Being-for-Others" (or, to use the English expression that is closer to the French, *pour-autrui*, "being-for-another") [137]. Actually, Sartre almost never ventures beyond a simple dyad, that is, a one-to-one relationship, in this section. His key concept is "the look"; through an analysis of this commonplace phenomenon, whereby I am observed and objectified by someone else, we can come to understand both that I myself am in one sense an object in the world, with all the possibilities of alienation, humiliation, and worse that are entailed by that fact, and that I exist in the midst of other free agents. But when, finally, Sartre comes to try to deal with group phenomena, in which there are more than two individuals classifiable under some common label or engaged in some common enterprise, he produces only a very sketchy account of something that he calls "the us-object," exemplified by workers who come to see themselves as the objects of a collective, exploitative look by the anonymous capitalist class, and an even sketchier and less satisfactory account of "the we-subject," which he is anxious to dismiss as little better than a psychological illusion. Another way of seeing what his *Critique* is primarily about is to say that it is an extended effort to make up for the deficiencies of this earlier treatment.

The years of the German occupation of France during World War II, during which very period *Being and Nothingness* was first published, were decisive years in the development of Sartre's political consciousness. Immediately after the war, he was one of the cofounders of the journal *Les Temps modernes* (of which he later served as editor for many years), and he attempted to develop a political line that would take some of its inspiration from the brief prewar "Popular Front"—a mélange of non-Communist leftist parties and the Communists. *Les Temps modernes* soon came to exemplify the intellectual spirit of this idea—particularly as some of the earlier cofounders who even then were further to the right, such as Aron and Camus, dropped out— but the notion of creating a genuine political movement along these lines never had a chance. (This notion, of course, was recently revived in France, but it suffered another severe setback as the Communists and the socialists once again acknowledged irresolvable conflicts.) Those postwar years were when both political and intellectual Stalinism was at its zenith, and the French Communist party was among the most Stalinist of Western European parties. Sartre has always exerted a greater appeal on some intellectuals within the *Italian* Communist party, which has traditionally prided itself on being more democratic and open than the French, than on his French comrades.

Through his editorial efforts in connection with *Les Temps modernes*, Sartre wrote a great many political essays on events of the moment. The linkages between the positions he took in these essays and the ontology of *Being and Nothingness* were, if for the most part not contradictory, by no means very apparent. He became increasingly aware of the repressiveness of the supposedly liberal democratic regime in France, and his feelings of what could be called anti-anti-Communism reached their high-water mark at the outset of the Korean War, when he wrote a series of editorials called "The Communists and Peace" [139]. He was convinced that the North Korean invasion of the South had resulted from a deliberate American provocation, and it was in this spirit that he reaffirmed the historical and social link that he perceived between the Soviet Union, despite all its Stalinist deformations, and the oppressed workers in the capitalist and underdeveloped countries of the world. It was this series of editorials, which Sartre wrote while Maurice Merleau-Ponty was still co-editor of *Les Temps modernes* (but when, as it happened, he was away on an extended vacation), that prompted Merleau-Ponty's resignation and an all-but-final rupture of friendship between the two men. Merleau-Ponty subsequently wrote a long piece called "Sartre and Ultra-bolshevism" as the final chapter of *Adventures of the Dialectic* [105]. It was highly critical both of Sartre's continuing political efforts to align himself with the Communists while not actually joining them and of his alleged failure to develop a theory of the institutional and other structural social "mediations" in which we live and which form such important parts of our everyday lives, a failure which Merleau-Ponty saw as stemming from Sartre's extreme and overwhelming conception of the power of individual freedom. Another way of understanding what Sartre is doing in the *Critique* is to regard it as an answer to Merleau-Ponty's charge, an effort to elaborate a truly *social* theory that would yet remain fundamentally true to the conceptions of human freedom developed in the earlier Sartrean philosophy.

Retracing my steps for a moment to the late 1940s, to the period when Sartre's new career as a political essayist was in full swing, I would like to mention another short work that foreshadows some of his later developments as a social theorist, *Anti-Semite and Jew* [136]. What is most valuable about this book, in my opinion, is Sartre's success in explaining the phenomenon of racism in categories that are not dependent on any form of racial or ethnic determinism, or, in other words, on any notion that biology is destiny. He shows that it is the anti-Semite who creates the stereotype of "the Jew" as a means of implementing his own project of brutal dominance, but Sartre also ends up by stressing the inauthenticity of the classical liberal solution to the practical problems posed by racism, which in this instance would entail the Jew's attempting to renounce and abandon his Jewishness on the ground that we are all members of the same, universal humanity. Some of what Sartre says toward the end of this work apropos of the Jewish question is a remarkable anticipation of the evolution of black consciousness in the United States from the late 1950s to the late 1960s, from the demands for strict equality to the slogans of black power and the real new sense of black pride.

One more point needs to be recalled, before I leave the 1940s, in my effort to retrace a few of the main steps in Sartre's development as a social theorist. There were two other important works written during this period, not by Sartre, but by his companion, Simone de Beauvoir. The works were, as noted in chapter one, *The Ethics of Ambiguity* and *The Second Sex*. Both must be judged as landmarks in the evolution of Sartre's thought, since, although they are de Beauvoir's and not Sartre's and contain many differences from his own writings with respect to nuance and areas of interest, they were books to which he apparently made important contributions as a critic while they were being written, just as all of his works have profited from similar services performed by her. (At least that is what they both claim about their very long relationship, and I believe it to be so.) Both books contain a number of strong theoretical claims, notably in their insistence on human solidarity as an ideal. De Beauvoir consistently argues, across relatively minor changes in her thinking, that no one will be fully free as long as one class or sex or other group is not.

The late 1950s was the period during which *Search for a Method* and the bulk of the *Critique* were written. Politically speaking, it was in one way a hopeful period: the post-Stalin thaw occurred under the new Soviet leadership of Nikita Khrushchev, and it was as a byproduct of that thaw that the editors of the Polish journal *Tworczosc* invited Sartre to contribute to a special issue on Marxism and modern France the first version of the essay that goes by the English title *Search for a Method*. But it was during that very year of the publication of this essay, 1956, that the incipient democratization that had been taking place all over Eastern Europe was brought to a premature halt, or at best was slowed to a crawl before being eventually reversed a few years later, by the Soviet invasion of Budapest. This was a traumatic time for Sartre, as it was for many of us; one of the immediate outcomes of it was his rather bitter editorial "The Ghost of Stalin" [148]. Moreover, in opposition to the stirrings of optimism occasioned by deStalinization, there was the dismal situation in which France found itself fighting an extremely brutal war against the Algerian people while trying to uphold the fiction that Algeria was an integral part of metropolitan France. It was a time of near despair for sensitive French people, and this helps explain Sartre's rather bizarre, desperate personal behavior during the period when he was completing the *Critique*.

The French edition of the *Critique* was published in 1960; the English translation of the bulk of the book first arrived on our shores only in late 1976, although *Search for a Method* had been available in translation for a number of years. Consequently, we are confronted with a certain cultural-lag phenomenon: Although some Americans and Britons delved into the French version long ago, it is not until very recently that the book has been available, realistically speaking, to most students in Anglo-Saxon countries. In France, on the other hand, it is commonly said the Sartre's works, naturally including the *Critique*, are phenomena of the past. The lightning-quick changes in the French intellectual weather have occurred once again; there are other fads now. So be it. If the *Critique* has something important to say to us, both about social theory and, because of that, about the times in which we live, then faddishness should not be our principal concern. I shall now summarize first *Search for a Method* and then the main points of the *Critique* proper.

The principal question in *Search for a Method* (actually entitled *Question de méthode*, "question of method," a more accurate title, I think) is whether we have the means today to construct a structural and historical anthropology. Sartre is, of course, using the word *anthropology* in its European meaning, "a science of man" (*man* in the generic sense). He says that we do have the means, and he suggests that the *Critique* proper might be considered a "Prolegomenon to Any Future Anthropology." In elaborating on what he is seeking and what the bases of his intellectual concerns are in *Search for a Method*, Sartre speaks in terms of three quite different traditions in modern social theory: American sociology, with its behaviorist and positivist orientation, the psychoanalytic approach to social explanation, which is most indebted to Freud, and finally Marxism. He clearly regards American social science as inimical to his purposes, but nevertheless a rather formidable opponent in its own way. It, along with the structuralist anthropology of Lévi-Strauss, about which he has much more to say in the *Critique*, is the best embodiment of what Sartre calls "analytic reason" or, quite often, "positivist reason." Sometimes he speaks as if dialectical reason should incorporate the methods and findings of positivist reason, which lay heavy stress on quantitativeness and calculation, into itself as a valuable but incomplete part of a larger methodological whole, but at other times Sartre places much more stress on the idea that positivism should simply be rejected. I think that there is a problem of consistency about his texts here, but I do not think that it is a very serious barrier to accepting other aspects of his social theory, because it is quite clear to me that the former approach— the view that analytic reason should be regarded as an auxilary and partial approach within dialectical thinking—is much sounder and more fruitful than the other.

As for Freudianism, Sartre finds much that is valuable in it in his brief remarks about it in *Search for a Method*. Here one has the impression that he is much less concerned with showing the shortcomings of Freud's implicit ontology, with its super-ego, ego, and id structures, than he was in *Being and Nothingness*, in which he was interested in elaborating on his own existential psychoanalysis. This same tendency in the later Sartre to be more at home with Freudian categories and methods and to worry less about Freud's primitive "ontology," as I have called it, is to be found also, I think, in *The Words*, Sartre's account of his childhood, and especially in *The Family Idiot*. The problem that the later Sartre finds with Freudianism is most of all its restriction of its methodology to the individual level, its neglect of the social.

And that is where Marxism comes in as a legitimate antidote and complement for Sartre. He says some very grand, eulogistic things about Marxism throughout *Search for a Method*, beginning with his opening claim that Marxism is the dominant and hitherto unsurpassable philosophy of our epoch. He speaks here of existentialism as an ideology that is parasitic upon the great epochal philosophy of Marxism, although he says that it was necessary for existentialism to develop on its own for some time because of the historical failure of post-Marxian Marxism to deal with problems of the human individual and its historical fate of having become rigidified and failing to develop for a long period. Very often I think that Sartre would have profited in *Search for a Method* by distinguishing between a Marxism$_1$ and a Marxism$_2$—the former being the ideal Marxism of Marx and, it is hoped, of the future, with which existentialism could become united, and the latter being the inept "orthodox" Marxism that has its roots in certain positivistic, scientistic tendencies particularly in Engels, and that has become the official Soviet version of the doctrine. I happen to agree very strongly with almost everything that Sartre says about Engels and the version of Marxism that he rejects, but in the bulk of his essay he calls this version, too, simply "Marxism," which is both confusing and inaccurate. As for the *ideal* Marxism, ideal particularly as a method or a set of heuristic suggestions, Sartre takes its concern with the formation of social groupings and its insight into the socioeconomic bases of historical events as valid and fundamental. It must be conjoined with the Freudian approach because, as Sartre puts it at one point, the so-called orthodox Marxists sometimes write as if they were "born at the age when we earn our first wages. They have forgotten their own childhoods." [153]

This, then, is Sartre's basic prescription for the crisis in social theory, as we find it in *Search for a Method:* One conjoins a Marxian approach to socioeconomic structures with a Freudian and existentialist attention to the individual as the source of free choice and, hence, (as expressed in Sartre's earlier work) as the creator of the life-world of meanings and values and structures, even of the very institutional structures that often oppress and overwhelm him or her. Put in this very brief way—and before we start attending to problems of detail—it strikes me, and indeed has always struck me since I first read the work, as an essentially sound formula for the social theory of the foreseeable future. Unfortunately, it has not yet met with widespread acceptance, either in the political West or in the East.

There are many other interesting themes in *Search for a Method,* but I shall neglect them in favor of moving on to the *Critique* proper. The *Critique,* the one volume of it that we have, has a very definite structure to it. After a difficult introductory section, in which Sartre develops the notion of dialectical method in opposition to analytic reason and provides a much more detailed critique of Engels, the volume consists of two long "books," the first of which is entitled "From Individual Praxis to the Practico-Inert" and the second of which bears the title "From Groups to History." Many of the titles of shorter subsections within the English translation of the *Critique* were added by the translator and editor, but these two are Sartre's own. An explication of them should provide a sense of the overall structure of the volume, which is quite clear-cut, even though sometimes obscured by Sartre's verbiage.

Individual *praxis,* or free dialectical activity, remains the basis, for Sartre, of all human society and history. *Praxis* is creative and productive; in our world, it labors under the necessity of satisfying needs under conditions of *scarcity.* What is scarce is matter, which is an antidialectical element. In working on scarce matter, individuals bring some of its characteristics, so to speak, into the human world, by virtue of the fact that they work together. But working together in this way is also a working apart, an alienated labor. Sartre's first illustration of the isolation of individuals in the typical work situation is a very good one: He, a bourgeois writer, is on vacation at a small hotel in the French countryside, and from out his hotel window he perceives the wall that separates the hotel's property from the country road. Within the hotel property, a gardener is working on the garden, while on the road a road-maintenance worker is making some repairs. The workers do not see each other at all and may not know each other, and neither may ever come to know that the other was there on that day. But there is a reciprocity between them that, by virtue of their positions in the class structure of French society, involves there being greater common ground between the two of them than between Sartre and either one. Yet Sartre, by observing, serves as a mediating third party between them; and his observation can be the basis of many reflections upon the structures of our society.

For Sartre, the condition of most of us in our daily lives is one of what he calls seriality, a collective existence that is, though collective, nevertheless profoundly alienated. This is what he means by the domain of the practico-inert: the inertness of matter has penetrated the very means by which we exercise our free *praxis*, thereby rendering it unfree in its very exercise. It should be remembered that the first book of the *Critique* is entitled "From Individual Praxis to the Practico-Inert." But individuals in our world never really, for all intents and purposes, live in isolation, so that to conceive of the isolated individual working on matter by himself or herself is, of course, a complete abstraction. Sartre readily admits and even stresses this. The domain of the practico-inert, wherein we exist in serial collectivity, on the other hand, is the typical domain of everyday life, as Sartre's several brilliant phenomenological descriptions of examples of it show us very well— the listeners to a government radio broadcast, the queue waiting for the bus at an urban bus stop in the morning, the workings of the "free market" in economics, and so forth.

There exists, however, the possibility of another form of common activity, a form that, at its purest, is unalienated. This is what Sartre calls the *group*, in radical distinction to seriality. The group is characterized by *common* praxis—an activity that, Sartre insists, must never be understood on the model of an organism, but must always be understood as *constituted* by the individual *praxis*. The activity of the group is a free totalization, or movement towards the achievement of a common project. Sartre sees the genesis of such group activity as being due to the fear of a threat from outside the collective in which the group is generated. The illustration that dominates his description of the fusion of a group is the action taken by residents of the section of Paris known as the Quartier St. Antoine who, under threat of being massacred by the royal soldiers, banded together to capture the Bastille near the outset of what we now call the French Revolution.

The entire second half of the published portion of Sartre's *Critique* is given over to a sort of preparation for his treatment of history; hence its title, "From Groups to History." Sartre wants to consider history as one large movement of totalization never to be completed in the form of what he calls a totality—a finished, fixed whole—but always moving *toward* some common outcome. Unfortunately, the demonstration of the validity of regarding history this way, despite all the backings and slidings and apparent irrationalities and unevenesses of history as we experience it, was supposed to have been given in volume two; and volume two, as I have indicated, remains unpublished and at best very unfinished even in its draft form. By the end of volume one, at any rate, Sartre has given us much material to contemplate that would militate *against* history's ever having a favorable outcome, in the sense of an overcoming either of material scarcity or of serial alienation and impotence within human collectives. He points out that members of a successful group will feel the need to retain their togetherness against the possibility of a recurrence of the external threat that unified them in the first place; the way in which this felt need is satisfied, Sartre shows, is through an implicit or explicit *pledge* that the members make to the effect that they will not backslide or betray one another. This pledge, he further shows, involves a sort of internalization of the fear that had united them; each member freely swears that he will become the object of terrorization by the others if he should ever violate the terms of the pledge and turn against his brothers. Thus Sartre calls this phenomenon "Fraternity-Terror," a Janus-faced reality that is at least implicit, if not explicit, in the common action of all serious sworn, or pledged, groups. The

pledge is the beginning of a potentially long process of organization within the group—the assignment of tasks, the division of labor, and so on— which reintroduces all sorts of new
forms of passivity into it and may eventually lead to institu-
tionalization and even bureaucracy at its worst. Of course,
Sartre always had in mind, when writing this, the bureaucrati-
zation of the Soviet Communist Party and government that
gradually set in within the Soviet Union after the Russian
Revolution. In short, Sartre provides much ground for pessimism about the future, at least in the terms in which he has
posed the problem of history; but he obviously also wants to
hold out the alternative possibility of amelioration, in the suppression of passivity and an upsurge of free activity on the part
of human groupings acting together.

Before turning to fundamental critical issues within the theory of the *Critique*, I wish briefly to update Sartre's development from the time of its publication to the present. The most
important intellectual event in his life during this period was
the publication of his *The Family Idiot*, which is a three-volume
study of the life of Gustave Flaubert [149]. It too, is incomplete;
there should have been a fourth volume that analyzed Flaubert's great classic novel, *Madame Bovary*, but it was never written. Sartre says, probably with considerable truth, that anyone
who understood Sartre's method of approach and was familiar
with the novel could write the fourth volume him- or herself.
The length of the Flaubert study is far greater than that of the
Critique—more than twenty-eight hundred pages of text. What
it does is carry out the program to which Sartre had already
pointed in *Search for a Method* when referring to Flaubert as an
illustration of the general problem of how to *explain* a given
individual's having become a great writer (or whatever), even
when one knows all that there is to know about the social and
cultural environment in which he or she was born and grew
up. *The Family Idiot* is intended to illustrate the new "method"
of which Sartre was speaking. I think it does so rather well, but
there are some qualifications. For one thing, the description of
the early childhood, the juvenilia, the family circumstances,
the high-school education, and so on of the younger and somewhat disregarded Flaubert brother, Gustave, is disproportion-
ately long compared with Sartre's attempt to integrate these
personal aspects of Flaubert's life with the French social struc-

ture of the early and mid-nineteenth century. This synthesis, or integration, occurs only in the third volume, which is by far the shortest. Of course, it still runs to 650 pages! And that leads to my second critical comment, which should be obvious: If Sartre's method can be carried out well only by devoting several thousands of pages to analyzing the case of one single individual, then that does not bode well for the future employment of the method by very many other writers, even by those who may agree with Sartre concerning its superiority. I do not think it essential to go on at such length in order to achieve a level of social understanding that is superior to the levels achieved by the separate alternative methods of human science that Sartre criticized in *Search for a Method*—American behaviorism, Freudianism, and so-called orthodox Marxism. Sartre has set a poor initial example simply in his prolixity.

While *The Family Idiot* was being completed, in the late sixties and early seventies, Sartre went through a period of political activity on the extreme Left, involving himself with a group known as the Maoists. The connection between their ideological position and the thought of Mao Tse-tung was not a close one, but no matter. In April 1970 Sartre took over the editorship of their newspaper, *La Cause du peuple*, when the original editor was jailed by the government, and there is a famous photograph of him distributing copies at a factory gate. Soon thereafter, his health took a decided downward turn, and he is now quite invalided, able to see only shapes. The one final point of interest about Sartre's most recent development is the fact, still relatively little known by the public outside of France, that Sartre no longer considers himself a Marxist. Although he does not repudiate the major contents of the *Critique*, he now feels that the identification that he made there between his position and Marxism was mistaken, because he feels that there is no room in the latter for the extraordinary emphasis that he places on the role of human freedom in both individual and social activity. He believes that Marxism is becoming outmoded owing to the changing character of capitalism, which has become the capitalism of the international oil cartels and other monopolies and hence has very little in common, in his opinion, with the capitalism that Marx confronted in the nineteenth century—very little except, perhaps, that both capitalisms are equally crushing with respect to the exercise of human freedom. I believe that Sartre is mistaken both in his view of the incompatibility of Marxism and some philosophy, if not in every respect Sartre's philosophy, that accords a considerable role to human freedom in social agency, and in his view about the outmodedness of Marx's analyses in light of the changing character of capitalist institutions. What concerns me in this chapter, however, is not an exegesis of Marx but an exegesis of Sartre, with a view to assessing his contribution to social theory.

My schema for the second, or critical, half of this exegesis is as follows. First, I will offer a few specific areas of contrast between what Sartre has done in his social theory, centering on the *Critique*, and certain major themes and problem areas of past political theories, notably those of Marx, Rousseau, and Hegel. Here I shall be most interested in spelling out both contrasts and similarities, but I shall also be offering tentative suggestions as to why Sartre's work appears to me to be an advance over the earlier theories, at least in principle if not in the actual way in which Sartre himself has worked out his ideas. (For I admit that his language is often overly complicated and he is not sufficiently disciplined in the organization and presentation of his material.) Secondly, I shall consider a few areas that seem to me to constitute some of Sartre's most serious philosophical problems as a social theorist.

At the beginning of this chapter I referred to Hegel's claim that the truth about the state and law and ethics was old, and needed only a clear formulation. Sartre, I stated, would never say this, but I maintained that a good case could be made for the existence of many continuities between Sartre's thought about society and earlier theories, and that this was not a bad thing. By "continuities," I do not, of course, mean just "agreements"; rather, a continuity in my sense may exist where an earlier theorist has defined certain questions as most important and in need of an answer within the domain being investigated, in this case society and politics, and a later theorist also treats those questions as important, even when his or her answer differs from that of the earlier thinker.

One of the most common claims made by the majority of social and political theorists over the centuries is that a social or political philosophy must be based on a prior theory of human nature. We can only understand how society works, it is said, if we first understand how the individuals who compose it work. We can immediately surmise that Sartre will be placed in a peculiar position vis-à-vis this question, if we know anything about his thought, because he is famous for denying that there is any such thing as a fixed human nature [147]. And he has not retracted that denial in his later work.

But what Sartre has done in the *Critique* is furnish us with a systematic social theory that avoids making any assumptions about a so-called human nature except the one crucial assumption that has been the focus of his entire career, namely, that human beings are, essentially, free creative activity, which he here calls by the Marxian term *praxis*. There is a large secondary literature on the subject of whether this tremendously important assumption does not constitute, after all, a theory about human nature, or at least an existential a priori. Of course in a sense it does. But it seems to me more important to see just what Sartre is trying to get at by his claim that there is no fixed human nature than to concern oneself excessively with the literal truth or falsehood of that simple statement, for a large part of this dispute seems to be clearly terminological. The important point, to me, about Sartre's way of constructing an account of social institutions and social change in the *Critique* is that he avoids making reference to the kinds of lists of supposedly universal qualities or attributes in human beings upon which human-nature-based social theories rely. I mean, for example, faculty psychologies that distinguish between an intellect and a will, or the assumptions of classical philosophies about the existence of certain definite and definable virtues and vices, or the medieval notion of an unchangeable natural law, which each rational human being is in principle capable of coming to know, or the bourgeois economic theorists' assumptions of innate egotism and commitment to self-interest, or some modern anthropologists' ideas about innate territorial imperatives or aggressive instincts. One problem with all such approaches is that they make it difficult to imagine a society in which people act very differently from the way they have acted at a certain time in the past or in the present, hence rendering it difficult to conceive of radical social change. And yet radical social change is a historical reality; it has occurred. Another problem is that such approaches force descriptions of all human actions to conform to the theoretical presuppositions; if an economist of the kind I have mentioned is provided with an instance of an apparently altruistic social action, for example, he or she will feel obliged to find some way of showing that it was really egotistic, after all. In short, assumptions, whether made by classical philosophers or modern social scientists, about a fixed human nature often preclude, when applied to social events, our understanding of *novel* developments. Yet novelty is a reality in our world, even if *absolute* novelty is not. One manifestation of this problem is the extreme discrepancy, noted even by their proponents, between the pretensions of being able to make concrete historical *predictions* that are an important part of most scientifically oriented modern political and social theories, on the one hand, and the paucity of actual attempts at making even modest predictions, on the other.

Now Sartre's approach, which, as I have said, derives from his early preoccupation with this question of human nature, has an open-endedness that avoids the pitfalls to which his opponents are prone. He does not pretend to tell us how the future is going to turn out; how could he, given his presuppositions about human freedom? And yet at the same time he has provided us with a very comprehensive framework for understanding social events as they occur. His analysis of the structures of human freedom in *Being and Nothingness* already showed us the ineluctable phenomenon of *lack* as fundamental; now, in the *Critique*, Sartre shows us the relationship between this fundamental structure and the reality of *need*, as need determines the general directions to be taken by human *praxis* in a world of material scarcity. *Scarcity*, for Sartre, is not a structure of human freedom; it is a contingent relationship between human reality and inert matter under the conditions of there not being enough matter for everyone. There are problems, to which I shall return later, with Sartre's conception of scarcity, but his views about its contingency give rise to some very interesting speculation on his part about possible worlds in which free beings might live without scarcity—indeed, about our own world's possibly becoming such a place in the distant future. The few sentences in which he engages in this speculation [140] provide the sort of liberating influence on the reader's social imagination that is exerted by the best of utopian or modern-science-fiction literature, without at the same time tempting the reader to believe that our own world of scarcity is anything like the world of utopian fantasy.

What Sartre has done with respect to the traditional question of whether a philosophy of human nature is required as the basis for social theory is essentially to agree with Marx's famous remark, in the sixth of his *Theses on Feuerbach*, to the effect that human nature or essence is nothing more than the ensemble of social relationships at a given time and place, yet Sartre avoids the anti-philosophical implication that at least some readers have drawn from what Marx says here. The implication to which I am referring is that one cannot have any social *philosophy* at all, because one is justified only in talking about the configurations of a given historical mode of production and not in talking about what features of human existence might be common to any two historical modes. Sartre in the *Critique*, on the contrary, is giving us a sort of ontology—it is an extension of the ontology of *Being and Nothingness*, though with a substitution of such basic terms as *"praxis"* for "being-for-itself" and "inert matter" for "being-in-itself"—which is intended to be specific to the human social world as it has existed from very primitive times right up to the present, though not necessarily into the indefinite future. So he does essentially what those who insist that a social philosophy be grounded in a so-called philosophy of man want done, but without the undesirable presuppositions about a fixed human nature.

A concomitant contribution of Sartre's, to which I have already referred but without stressing it, is his success in demonstrating the value of a historical materialist set of assumptions about the course of history—what makes history happen—without presupposing a flat positivistic metaphysical materialism of the sort incorporated in Engels's notion of a dialectics of nature and in Lenin's famous essay *Materialism and Empirio-Criticism* [67]. There are hints of the same dubious scientistic metaphysics in some of Marx's later writings, particularly in the preface to *Capital*, in which he speaks of his having discovered the laws of the natural history of mankind and similar notions. Sartre has performed a particularly important service by demonstrating in detail, especially in the early pages of the *Critique*, the positivism latent in Engels's stipulating three "most general laws," as the latter expresses it, that constitute the basis of dialectical logic—the transformation of quantity into quality and the reverse, the negation of the negation, and the interpenetration of opposites—and which are apparently accepted as gospel in courses in dialectical materialism taught in the Soviet Union and countries closely allied with it. A great deal of the explanatory value of Marxism as a world view has been distorted as a result of this sort of approach. Sartre does not simply attack it, as others sympathetic to Marxism have done, but also he shows in some detail its incompatibility with genuinely nonpositivistic, genuinely dialectical thinking.

On another issue that is central to Marxist thought, the nature of class, Sartre also makes a very positive contribution. As is well known, Marx used the concept of class without ever defining it very clearly; the last volume of *Capital* trails off at the very point at which Marx was about to embark on a systematic exposition of classes, and we are left with about one and a half pages of this section. Many others, of course, have attempted to grapple with the definition of social class, but I think that Sartre is exceptionally successful in steering clear of the untenable idea of classes as rigid entities, on the one hand, and the equally inaccurate ideological contention that classes are no longer real or meaningful phenomena under modern capitalism. He shows the complexity of the phenomenon—the sense in which contemporary classes are mélanges of serial collectivities that have never been gathered into groups, and of groups in various stages of formation and deformation. His distinction, early in the book, between the interest of a dominant social class and the destiny, as he puts it, that a subordinate class experiences as its counterpart of the dominant class's interest clarifies the meaning of this idea of *interest* in a very important way. I have found many Marxists and other social theorists to be ambiguous or unclear about it; the notion of "interest" is an inheritance from Adam Smith and others in his line, and in its original context it is redolent of the idea that one's class position is, precisely, one's destiny, in the sense that it is that position which determines one's way of acting socially and economically. Thus, Marxists, for instance, will sometimes speak of the "interests of the working class." But if they are to be consistent they must admit that those interests, if they are such, are not at all of the same type as are the interests of capitalists, for the perspective within which Marx works demands that we admit the possibility of a future society whose workings will no longer be determined by the clash of opposing interests.

I could continue at greater length about some of the ties and contrasts between Sartre's social theory and Marxism—for instance, in Sartre's way of showing, both through his non-faculty-oriented ontology and by his choice of practical examples, the unity of theory and practice. But I would prefer instead, for purposes of a balanced presentation, to make explicit a few of the connections that I have found, and which Sartre himself almost never makes explicit, between the social theory of the *Critique* and two other philosophers and philosophical traditions.

First, there is Rousseau. In Simone de Beauvoir's autobiography, *Memoirs of a Dutiful Daughter* [34], she mentions the great enthusiasm that Sartre showed for Rousseau's philosophy during one of Sartre and de Beauvoir's early meetings. It was a graduate student's enthusiasm during a formative period; I do not mean to imply that Sartre's whole philosophy, for the rest of his career, should be understood as a Rousseauism *caché*. But it is certainly the case that the *Critique,* though I do not know of a single explicit reference to Rousseau throughout the book, is highly evocative of problems and even of imagery that can best be related to Rousseau's social philosophy. For instance, one of Rousseau's best-known and most provocative phrases in *The Social Contract* is "forced to be free," which is usually cited out of context. In Rousseau's terms the individual who has entered into the contract and agreed to act in accordance with what the general will determines to be right may later backslide and attempt to act otherwise, that is, in plain language, to commit a crime. But to do so would, for Rousseau, violate the original terms of the contract under which the individual exchanged the arbitrary obedience to impulse that characterizes people in the state of nature for the moral liberty that first comes into existence in a political community; hence, when that community prohibits such backsliding, it is forcing the individual to be free.

Something very much like this takes place in Sartre's analysis of the dual phenomenon of "Fraternity-Terror," as he puts it, that characterizes "the pledged group." Of course there are very significant differences, too. The pledge, or oath, is Sartre's substitute for the old notion of a social contract. The important

difference about Sartre's idea, as opposed to that of the classical social-contract theorists, is that the pledge is not to be understood on the model of an exchange transaction, like a buy-
ing-and-selling, but rather dialectically, as a result of the
group's felt need, in the presence of some external threat, to
give itself permanence and for each individual member to serve
as a mediating third party bearing witness to the reciprocity
that obtains, and is now promised for the indefinite future,
between all pairs of other members of the group. In other
words, to put it schematically and abstractly, Sartre sees the
pledge as essentially a triadic, not merely a dyadic, phenomenon. What Sartre sees the pledge as doing is internalizing,
within the group, the fear that each individual felt, before the
group was fused, vis-à-vis the external menace—the fear that
in fact motivated the group to form in the first place. This
internalization of fear, as brotherhood and terror within the
group, expresses itself as each individual's declared willingness
to become the object of the group's wrath and revenge if at any
future time he should betray his brothers. This is not a warm-
hearted picture of an analytically rational, businesslike agreement, such as one gets from the accounts of the social contract
in Locke or even, though with important differences from
Locke that anticipate Sartre, in Rousseau. Sartre is attempting,
here as elsewhere in the *Critique*, to elucidate the foundations
of our social world as we live in it under a regime of scarcity,
and indeed his account *does* elucidate both the dark side and
the brighter side of all sorts of human communities as we read
about them in history and experience them for ourselves, from
primitive tribes to modern times. Certainly, for example, the
events surrounding Stalinist terror, which Merleau-Ponty had
already dealt with so interestingly in his book *Humanism and
Terror*, [106] are never far from Sartre's consciousness, and
neither are the events surrounding the French Revolution. But
his account of the pledge is also intended to illuminate less
extraordinary events, that is, interractions within small groups
committed to achieving very limited objectives.

Sartre does not depart from the basic Rousseauan idea that
there exists within the group a new and real freedom that did
not exist before, in the previously alienated condition of the
individuals living in what Sartre calls "seriality." But he does
not quite go along with the Rousseauan dictum that it is within

the group that *morality* is achieved—as if what is moral were prescribed in advance, in the nature of things. Rather, for Sartre, as everyone who is familiar with his thought realizes, values are *created*, generated, by human beings. But now, in the *Critique*, his account of the group enables us to see much better than in his earlier writings just how groups go about generating values that are simultaneously internalized, perhaps later to be revised or entirely rejected, by individual members. He does not say a great deal explicitly about values, but the *Critique* contains a very long and remarkable footnote [141] on the subject and another equally important footnote [142] on how people who are born into a group recommit themselves, in a kind of rebirth, through such ceremonies as, in the case of religious groups, baptism. These passages in particular help provide a framework, not for a Sartrean ethics, because in an important sense there is and can be no such thing, but for a Sartrean account of ethical phenomena that in one way is a return to Rousseau from Kant (because it was Kant who made into a formula for the *individual* what Rousseau had intended as a formula for understanding the notion of a human *community*, namely, that "obedience to the law one has prescribed to oneself is freedom"), and in another way repudiates Rousseau by repudiating most of his strong moralism.

Hegel is another social and political philosopher (the last whom I shall treat here) to whom Sartre's *Critique* provides very interesting similarities and contrasts. In Hegel's case, unlike that of Rousseau, Sartre does draw explicit attention to comparisons on several occasions, but he does little to elaborate on them. Pietro Chiodi, whose book on the *Critique* has been translated into English from the Italian [26], is critical of Sartre for, essentially, relapsing into Hegelianism from Marxism. Chiodi makes a good case, and Sartre's recent rejection of Marxism, which I mentioned earlier, lends credence to Chiodi's point. Chiodi concentrates, and rightly so with respect to the relationship between Sartre and Hegel, on the question of *alienation*. Sartre certainly does wish, in the *Critique*, to show that the basis of alienation in human society is otherness, or alterity. Anyone familiar with Sartre's account of "the look" as the basis of the phenomenon of "being-for-another" in *Being and Nothingness* will realize that it would be very hard for Sartre, short of totally repudiating his earlier perspective, to develop a social theory in which there exists any possibility, even of the remotest kind, of human beings' overcoming all forms of alienation for even a split second! But, as a medieval philosopher would say, we must *distinguish*—we must distinguish various senses of *alienation*. One sense refers to the universal human phenomenon of ineluctable, and fundamentally *physical*, otherness; another sense of *alienation* refers to phenomena peculiar to the capitalist mode of production, and it is not to be found, for instance, in the feudal society of the Middle Ages; and there are probably other senses of the word that are intermediate between these two. Sartre makes such distinctions explicitly; he even refers—as Marx did in his chapter on the "Fetishism of Commodities" in *Capital*—to the difference between alienation under capitalism and the somewhat equivalent phenomenon in the less commodity-dominated medieval society [143].

So when, in the *Critique*, Sartre concludes a section in which he has shown the pervasiveness of the first-mentioned kind of alienation in all human collectivities, he asks openly whether this account constitutes a return to Hegel, presumably *from* Marx [144], and he answers, correctly, "Both yes and no." This question of the meanings of alienation is a very complex one in Sartre's work, as it is in both Hegel and Marx, of course, and a thorough treatment of it would require several volumes. However, the importance of it for understanding the ultimate thrust of Sartre's theory can be put very simply, as follows: If his theoretical framework really commits him, as Chiodi and some other critics seem to be claiming, to the view that there is no way of *ever* overcoming alienation in any significant form under any conditions, then indeed Sartre is repudiating the commitment to the possibility of genuine revolutionary change in history that we find in the Marxist tradition, and he is reaffirming the political and philosophical conservatism that is implicit throughout Hegel's work, only without the sense of the present as being optimal that we find in Hegel. However, I do not believe that this is an accurate account of the terminal point of the *Critique*. It seems clear to me (as it did to the writer of a doctoral dissertation who examined the matter in considerable detail [159]) that Sartre remains strongly committed to the idea that a nonalienated society, in some important senses of *alienation*, is a real possibility.

On another crucial issue, however, Sartre's distance from Hegel is very explicit throughout the *Critique* and not at all difficult to resolve—the issue of the *nature* of the group, whether it is in any sense an organism. Here, in my opinion, Sartre is especially illuminating: his entire analysis is devoted to showing that the constitutive dialectical activity of individual human *praxis* is organic—we ourselves are organisms—but that what he calls the *constituted* dialectic, the activity of the group, is not organic. What gives his treatment special historical importance is, of course, that Sartre is constantly affirming his commitment to the dialectical tradition in philosophy, to the dialectical as opposed to the analytic way of looking at the social world. Now, it would be nothing startling to read someone in the analytic tradition, from Locke on, denouncing the metaphor of organism as applied to states and other political communities (although, as an aside, we ought to recall that the work of the father of this tradition in British political philosophy, Hobbes's *Leviathan*, is pervaded by just such a metaphor). But the dialectical tradition, both in the work of Hegel and also more recently and rather more crudely in the writings of F. H. Bradley and particularly Bernard Bosanquet, has tended to identify itself with this key idea, that human communities are somehow entities of a higher order of reality than are individual human beings. Even in the case of Marx, who I believe can be shown to repudiate this idea quite thoroughly, there remains a real suspicion that perhaps he is an organicist at heart, because his later work focuses exclusively on the level of collectivities and fails to say anything much of value about the relationship of these social structures to the individuals who compose them. Sartre, however, both remains a thoroughgoing dialectician and shows, contrary to Hegel and so many others, that a dialectical world view does not require a theory of organicism.

There is yet another sense, as obvious as it is important, in which Sartre's theoretical framework constitutes a very significant departure from Hegel; it is Sartre's rejection, through undercutting by analysis, of Hegel's key theme that the modern State should be considered the supreme or normative form of social structure. Here, of course, it is the later Hegel, the Hegel of the *Philosophy of Right* and the *Philosophy of History*, of whom we have to think first and foremost; in his earlier years, in the

69

Phenomenology, he had attributed a greater supremacy to the religious community. Sartre's *Critique*, especially in its final half, stresses the extreme complexity of the structures of the modern social world: It is, as he correctly shows, a vast congeries of groups (in his technical sense of the word) at all stages of waxing and waning, and of frequently overlapping collectivities that are serial and hence alienated in various ways. He cannot accept the idea that a large modern nation can ever really become a group, and of course he is right. But this is, in effect, a detailed demonstration by Sartre of a point that I made in chapter one, namely, the need to think in terms of *social* philosophy or *social* theory rather than of purely *political* philosophy, *even if* one wishes to focus on the nature of certain specifically political institutions. A *Philosophy of Right* that focuses on the State is outmoded, even as it had begun to become in Hegel's own time; we need only recall Hegel's famous claim that philosophy can paint its gray on gray only when a form of life has become old. History has moved along and the world has changed, so that in a very important sense Hegel was wrong, after all, to imply, as he does in the passage that I cited at the beginning of this chapter, that the truth about right and ethics and the State is not only very old, but unchangeable. And yet there remain deep continuities between Hegel and Sartre.

I now wish to raise what I consider to be some of the most serious philosophical problems in Sartre's *Critique*—some of the greatest drawbacks to regarding it as in any sense definitive concerning the fundamental issues in social philosophy with which it deals. There are difficulties with his notion of methodology, particularly concerning the relationship between analytic and dialectical reason, which require further exploration but which I shall pass over in silence here. It is important to note, however, by way of introducing my first problem area, that in *Search for a Method* Sartre advocates what he calls a "progressive-regressive" method, of which the first volume of the *Critique* is presumably supposed to exemplify the regressive part. The progressive part, on the other hand, would be the reconstruction of history, based on the regressive analyses, that would have been undertaken in volume two of the *Cri-*

tique, had it been completed. Sartre says that the problem with a lot of so-called orthodox Marxist writing is that it has become lazy, that it has applied interpretations to history of a very cut-and-dried sort, without undertaking new regressive, or what might be called substructural, analyses, of the kind that Marx himself certainly did undertake.

With this as background, then, we may pose the following rather obvious question: If both Marx's and Sartre's analyses are in one sense or another regressive—and I can certainly make the case that this is an accurate way of seeing Marx's key theme of the contrast between the appearances of modern economic life, which he calls the sphere of circulation, and the underlying essence of the capitalist system, which he calls the sphere of production, in *Capital*—then why do they come up with such different theoretical results? We can rule out the answer that Sartre would claim that Marx was simply all wrong, because that is not at all what he says in the *Critique*, and it is not what he could consistently say even now that he has repudiated Marxism after his fashion. One partially satisfactory answer is that Sartre is attempting to give an analysis at a deeper, or more transhistorical level than Marx was in *Capital*. Marx was concentrating on one particular economic system, historically time-limited, and indeed his overarching purpose was precisely to show that this system *was* time-limited and *could* be superseded by a higher system contrary to what the bourgeois political economists maintained. On the other hand, Sartre in the *Critique*, it might be said, is concerned with showing the basis of such phenomena as alienation in any and all historical modes of production as they have existed or could exist under conditions of material scarcity. But then the problem is how to connect the kind of detailed economic analysis that Marx undertakes with the quasi-ontological, quasi-sociological level of Sartre's analysis. Sartre provides us with very few clues as to how to do this. He does offer a short discussion of exchanges on a free market as illustrating seriality, and toward the end of the book his lengthy analyses of the concept of class exhibit obvious affinities with Marxian theory. But, to put it as bluntly as possible, Sartre shows very little detailed sense of the *economic* aspects of socioeconomic structures. Production, exchange, and even *consumption* in the economic sense— all terms that are applicable both within and without capitalist systems—receive very little clarification in the *Critique* or anywhere else in Sartre's writings. So here we have identified one serious problem, the problem of the linkage between his type of analysis and the terminology that economic theorists, not only Marx but all others as well, are accustomed to employ. It is an important problem, because Sartre has on a number of occasions proclaimed his adherence to the principle that we do make history on the basis of our particular socioeconomic conditions [154].

There is a further problem that is implicit in what I have just written. It has to do with the *ontological* status of the phenomena that are basic to Sartre's analysis in the *Critique*—such things as *praxis* and the fused group. There is a passage in the *Critique* in which Sartre says:

> For those who have read *Being and Nothingness*, I can describe the foundation of necessity as practice: it is the For-Itself, as agent, revealing itself initially as inert or, at best, as practico-inert, in the milieu of the In-Itself. [144]

In *Being and Nothingness*, Sartre appeared as an ontologist in the grand tradition, even if the ontological ultimates of his system turned out to be, in important respects, inversions of the dominant conceptions of that tradition (a nonexistent God, nonsubstantival selves, and the attribution of massive, full being to those aspects of reality outside of thought or consciousness that had formerly been regarded as closest to nonbeing). From the above citation, it would seem that the *Critique*, too, must be seen as somehow heir to that same grand tradition. But this conception of the latter work conflicts with another conception both of the method and of the substance of what Sartre is doing in his later writings. Repeatedly, in *Search for a Method*, Sartre insists that the "living Marxism" of which he is in favor, as opposed to the dead-handed "orthodox" approach, is *heuristic*; that is, it eschews a priori categories. Both in that work and near the beginning of the *Critique* proper, he severely criticizes Friedrich Engels for generating the sort of Marxist metaphysics that he does (as I agree) in his *Dialectics of Nature*. Sartre's attitude in these passages appears to be rather antiontological.

There is, then, in my opinion, a basic ambiguity in Sartre's conception of what he, as a social theorist, has come to discover through his lengthy regressive analyses. Is their outcome to be construed as a set of ontological ultimates, valid for all times and places, at least within the world of human beings as it has existed up to now? Or rather, is that outcome another contribution, perhaps of great heuristic value, to the new type of explanation of society that is called for in *Search for a Method*, offered without pretensions to exclusive validity as an ontology?

The ambiguity concerning the intended significance of Sartre's social theory can be pinpointed by concentrating for a moment on one of his putative ontological ultimates, *praxis*. Sartre begins with it, in the *Critique*, in its most nearly pure state: as individual *praxis* operating on inert matter. He is thoroughly aware of Marx's fundamental objections to the "Robinsonades," the stories of Robinson Crusoe on his desert island, which the bourgeois political economists were so fond of using as points of departure for their lessons about the supposedly constant features of *homo oeconomicus*: as it is easy to show in most cases, the writers have surreptitiously introduced characteristics peculiar to the system of capitalism into their descriptions, thus destroying their scientific value. Sartre's most important defense against the charge of resurrecting "Robinsonism" is, as I take it, that he has deliberately chosen to begin his analysis at the furthest limits of *abstraction* appropriate to his subject matter, human society; the entire published volume of the *Critique* is intended to be a movement from abstract to concrete levels of analysis. (Thus, the theoretical context within which he speaks, completely impersonally, of his isolated actor is entirely different from that within which the economists were writing.) "Individual *praxis* operating on inert matter" is meant to name an abstract situation, not an actual or possible historical one. But then, why should the term, *praxis*, be considered more descriptive of an ultimate reality or of a limiting case than let us say, *practice* or *labor* or, alternatively, *being-for-itself*? It is simply a matter of names, it will be answered; *praxis* has past and present historical connotations, including connotations derived from the history of thought, that make it a preferable word to use for Sartre's purposes in the *Critique*. The connotations are very important; for instance, to shift from describing the career of being-for-itself to describing that of *praxis* is to signal a change of emphasis in one's predominant conception of human reality, a change from the orientation

73

toward consciousness or intellect that characterizes the contemplative tradition of earlier mainstream Western philosophy to the orientation toward activity that characterizes Marxism and some other modern movements. Nevertheless, the two terms *being-for-itself* and *praxis* presumably do not denote two denumerably different entities or kinds of entities.

If this is the case, as I assume it to be, then *praxis* is a very general term indeed, and the variety of its potential specific contents appears to be nearly endless. *Praxis* has, it may be conceded, proved useful to Sartre as an omnipresent, unifying category in the *Critique,* but one is forced to question whether it will prove similarly useful to any other social theorist or, in fact, even to Sartre himself in any other place. In any case, I can see no way of demonstrating the necessity of its being similarly useful to all future social theories. As far as I can determine, *The Family Idiot* would not have been greatly altered in content if its author had refused to allow himself to use either *praxis* or any synonym of equal generality and technicality in the places where it now appears. These considerations put in doubt any claims that might be made or implied concerning the status of the results of Sartre's regressive analysis in the *Critique* as a definitive ontology.

Another problem area in Sartre's social theory is that of causality, or, to put it in another seemingly very different but in fact closely related way, the problem of the opposition between human activity and nature. Some version of these problems affects in one way or another every writer within the phenomenological tradition, and the result is often a very fruitful one. So it is with Sartre. Nature, for all he knows, may be the domain of the determinism, but culture, the human social world, can be described and accounted for in noncausal terms. This does not mean, of course, that free human *praxis* does not *do* things, bring about changes, and so on; of course it does. And sometimes it fails because of the inertness of matter; to use the simplest kind of example, without the proper tools we cannot move mountains no matter how much we may wish to. But Sartrean *praxis,* transparent free action, while it is in a certain sense material, in another sense it is not; it transcends matter, which by definition for Sartre is inert. He is able to go quite far with this way of accounting for human action, both in his earlier and in his later work, and of course a number of commentators, among whom Anthony Manser [92] is especially prominent, have shown that this is a valuable point at which to bring together aspects of Sartre's philosophy with some of the literature of action theory in the analytical tradition. In the last analysis, however, I think that he runs into problems by virtue of his steadfast refusal to attribute any causal efficacy whatsoever to nonhuman, or at least inorganic, phenomena: the weather that produces a bad harvest and temporarily ruins a country, the epidemic that sweeps through the Athenian city-state during the Peloponnesian War and decimates the population, and so on.

Of course, he can also show how such phenomena may be treated as what, in his earlier work, he calls "coefficients of adversity" on the basis of which human *praxis* acts. In fact, the early pages of the *Critique* contain a very interesting and convincing illustration of this in the form of an analysis of how the seasonal flooding of the Yellow River, which is basic to the social life of large areas of China even to this day, was the outcome of the ancient Chinese peasants' practice over a period of centuries of indiscriminately felling trees along the riverbanks. Still, this illustration is not totally convincing. Some ruinous floods do *not* seem attributable to human agency, however remote. Moreover, there is considerable ambiguity about Sartre's treatment of nonhuman organisms, meaning, essentially, animals. Are *they* characterized by *praxis?* His answer seems to be that undoubtedly *praxis* does characterize animals, but that he has said very little about them throughout his writings because he really does not understand them very well.

In short, a large cluster of problems surrounds the Cartesian, Kantian, and Hegelian opposition between human beings and nature, to which Sartre clings even in his *Critique.* I think that it is ultimately a serious defect in his book, although I am not prepared at this time to offer a detailed account of how a version of Sartre's social theory that had undergone radical alteration along these lines would look. Let me simply say that one approach to such an alteration would be to begin by treating "inert matter" as an abstract, limiting concept rather than a real entity, just as I have suggested in the case of *praxis.*

Another serious problem area in the *Critique,* upon which quite a number of commentators have come to focus, is the great emphasis that Sartre places on the concept of "scarcity" as a major explanatory factor. I have discussed this at greater length elsewhere [86]. The basic problem is that the term is inherently quite vague, and, in order to begin to make some sense of it, we must be able to form some conception of what a state of affairs opposite to one of scarcity (that is, "abundance") would be like. Recent events have, it seems to me, cast doubt on our ability to do so. Here is a superficial question, but an important one: Was the condition of the majority of, let us say, the population of the United States in the early 1960s, the period when the slogan "the affluent society" was so widely bantered about, truly one of comparative abundance? Or was the widespread belief that this was the case simply an illusion? I suspect that the latter is more correct, but if so then we must confront the problem of *defining* "scarcity." For the *fact* of conspicuous consumption in the early 1960s was *not* simply an illusion: in the society in question, at least, there was enough, and more than enough, of matter of many kinds—food, clothing, and building materials, to begin with, and such other items as energy sources besides. Wastage was vast. What was happening? What has happened?

"Scarcity" is a relative term, as is "need." Marx insisted on this in many pages of *Capital*, and it was the widespread failure to take this point seriously that led, probably more than any other factor, to the Bernsteinian "revision" of Marx (on the grounds that Marx's alleged predictions of increasing impoverishment of the working class had been falsified) in the late nineteenth century. There can be no satisfactory quantitative measure of scarcity, as there can be of such items as necessary labor time or the rate of surplus value; to require such a measure in the case of scarcity is to demand the impossible. However, simply because it cannot be totally quantified the concept of "scarcity" is not therefore to be considered meaningless; far from it. But the issue that these facts raise for Sartre's social theory is whether it was advisable to lay so much of the weight of explanation on this concept and on the alternative possibility of a scarcity-free social world of the future.

In the classical Marxism of Marx, particularly in *Capital* and his other later works, it seems to me no single concept is allowed to play as decisive a role in distinguishing between the structures of past and present societies and that of a projected future socialist society as does "scarcity" in Sartre's *Critique*. "Class division" comes closest, perhaps, but unfortunately *Capital* breaks off just at the point where Marx is beginning to analyze the concept of "class." By contrast with a capitalist system, it may be said, Marx's socialist society would be one in which the exploitation of workers by means of forcing them to produce surplus value would have ceased, and *this* is a decisive difference; true, but Marx himself often stressed that surplus labor— that is, labor beyond the amount needed to reproduce the workers' means of subsistence (itself now redefined so as to allow everyone to maintain a *relatively* abundant living standard)—would still exist under socialism, in order to make possible planning and reinvestment toward the future. For Marx, a large network of interrelated concepts, some of them quite complex and dependent for their meanings on concrete details of present-day society, must be brought to bear to draw the contrast between presocialist and socialist structures. Too often in Sartre's *Critique*, on the other hand, "scarcity" and its elimination seem to have been given a unique importance in establishing this contrast. It is no doubt partly for this reason that Sartre encounters such great difficulties in speaking about the future. Of course we cannot press him too far on this point apropos of the published part of the *Critique*, because volume two was to have been the part that would view history as a long process of totalization and thus introduce the temporal dimensions, including presumably the future, into Sartre's social theory in a way in which they do not appear in volume one. But I think one can see with what kinds of issues he would need to deal in order to try to render more satisfactory his use, which I believe to be excessive, of "scarcity" as an explanatory concept.

My final general area of criticism of Sartre's social theory centers on his pivotal account of the "fused group," as the English translation for some reason would have it, or of "the group in fusion," as the French version goes. There is a sense in which Sartre takes this kind of group to be normative—a sense that I shall try to explicate in a moment—and it is here that the problems, as I see them, lie. Let me begin by citing several sentences from Sartre's account of this, which, as I have mentioned, is illustrated by the taking of the Bastille by residents of the Parisian Quartier St. Antoine:

From this moment on, there is something which is neither group nor series, but what Malraux, in *Days of Hope*, called the Apocalypse—that is to say, the dissolution of the series into a fused group. And this group, though still unstructured, that is to say, entirely *amorphous*, is characterized by being the direct opposite of alterity. In a serial relation, in fact, unity as the formula (*Raison*) of the series is always *elsewhere*, whereas in the Apocalypse, though seriality still exists at least as a process which is about to disappear, and although it always may reappear, synthetic unity is always *here*. [145]

This high-water mark of incipient, perfervid revolutionary activity—group *praxis* at its limit (but so unique as to be irreducible, strictly speaking, to the status of a *group*)—is, in Sartre's own words, "not structured, . . . *amorphous*." Phenomena of this sort, or very nearly of this sort, may in fact have occurred and continue to occur from time to time in one society or another; Sartre's account is, from one point of view, simply an attempt to give a generalized description of them and to make such apparently structureless phenomena as intelligible as they can ever be made. But is it not in fact a mistake to say that any actual group in fusion—that is, any collective movement to break with old rules and restraints and to attempt to achieve novel social goals when in its initial phase of enthusiastic formation—is totally without structure? After all, the members will always have their individual histories, which they will carry with them, and their nascent common project, whatever it may be, will itself dictate certain simple, general lines of conduct along which the group must act in order to retain any hope of success. Moreover, whereas the apocalypse of religious myth is outside of time, no social group in fusion can ever operate totally outside of temporal limits.

If this is so, then Sartre's account of the group in fusion at its height can only be taken as an ideal-typical model, not as a generalized description that is *exactly* applicable to any particular historical event, past, present, or future. This has important implications for his social theory, particularly for that aspect of it that has to do with the possibility of revolutionary change in the direction of a socialist society. Any such change, if it should occur (and if, as I am inclined in my less cynical moments to concede, it already has occurred here and there in truncated form), would have to be radical and fundamental in order to be genuine, but it could not be Apocalyptic.

There is one other aspect of Sartre's account of the group in fusion that has caused considerable concern among some of his readers, and that is its normative force. Sartre does not, to be sure, explicitly present his group in fusion as a social norm to be striven for; he depicts such phenomena as being extremely ephemeral, and it is his clear intention throughout the *Critique* to avoid all moralizing and simply to describe various "social *ensembles*" in a certain conceptual order. He is, in fact, considerably more successful (in the *Critique*) at maintaining this peculiar combination of a strong, implicit, barely suppressed ethical commitment and a methodological ethical neutrality, which is characteristic of the Hegelian tradition, than is either Hegel or Marx himself. But if, as Sartre does say: "The worker will be saved from his destiny only if the human multiplicity as a whole is permanently changed into a group *praxis*" [146], and if the group in fusion is the limiting case of group *praxis*, it seems to follow that the group in fusion must play some sort of an ideal role in a normative, as well as in a conceptual, sense. This is dangerous because Sartre's group in fusion is by definition a *praxis* without theory. To treat it as being in any sense, however farfetched and removed from more ordinary human situations, a normative model for social activity is to appear to concede some truth to the false charges, often made by political reactionaries, that revolutionary activity is inherently mindless and that critical or revolutionary theory is basically antiintellectual.

It is paradoxical that a person of such intense intellectuality as Sartre should leave any opening within his theoretical framework for such implications to be drawn. I have no desire to press this final criticism, which is more impressionistic than textually demonstrable. The problem here stems from the interweaving of the normative with the descriptive—in fact, the refusal to accept the radical distinction between normative and descriptive that characterizes many other traditions of social philosophy and social science—that is so typical of a dialectical approach and which at the same time gives such an approach much of its force.

I shall be very brief about Sartre's ultimate contribution. Although the *Critique of Dialectical Reason* was being written twenty years ago, it is highly contemporary. It has transcended many of the shibboleths and illusions of past theories. It depicts the human world as it is, filled with violence [86], while at the same time showing the complex rationality that underlies such violence. It could easily be used, as Wilfrid Desan demonstrated in his book *The Marxism of Jean-Paul Sartre* [37], to shed theoretical light on the American civil-rights movement of the early 1960s. It proved to be an invaluable guide in comprehending the protest movements of the late 1960s and their generally anticlimactic aftermaths, through which we are now living. It will continue to be a source of understanding of contemporary social movements through all the vicissitudes that lie ahead in the near future. I have always thought so, and the many intrepid students with whom over the years I have worked through the formidable text of the *Critique* have been nearly unanimous in agreeing with me.

CHAPTER THREE

Injustices and Wrongs
Toward a New Emphasis in the
Philosophy of Law

Franz Kafka's novel *The Trial* includes a famous parable, which has been reprinted frequently in anthologies of different sorts, concerning the gateway to "the Law." Part of it reads as follows:

> Before the Law stands a doorkeeper. To this door-keeper there comes a man from the country who begs for admittance to the Law. But the doorkeeper says that he cannot admit the man at the moment. The man, on reflection, asks if he will be allowed, then, to enter later. "It is possible," answers the doorkeeper, "but not at this moment." Since the door leading into the Law stands open as usual and the doorkeeper steps to one side, the man bends down to peer through the entrance. When the doorkeeper sees that, he laughs and says, "If you are so strongly tempted, try to get in without my permission. But note that I am powerful. And I am only the lowest doorkeeper. From hall to hall, keepers stand at every door, one more powerful than the other. And the sight of the third man is already more than even I can stand." These are difficulties which the man from the country has not expected to meet. The Law, he thinks, should be accessible to every man and at all times, but when he looks more closely at the doorkeeper in his furred robe, with his huge pointed nose and long thin Tartar beard, he decides that he had better wait until he gets permission to enter. . . . [58]

There are, of course, many levels of meaning to this parable. Kafka himself, I am sure, intended it most of all as an exploration of the meaning of the law in the religious sense, as it is treated in the Judeo-Christian tradition. Kafka was familiar

81

with the Bible and the Talmud in particular, and the character in the novel who proclaims the parable to Joseph K., the anti-hero of the novel, is a priest. But in our tradition there has always been a close conceptual and historical connection between the law, in the sense of the law of God, and the law in the sense of the statutes and procedures that together constitute our judicial system. So Kafka's novel can also be taken as a parable about, and parody of, our Western legal systems, with the short parable in this chapter being an epitomization of what he has to say. If the parable applies with considerable force to the law as it is practiced, it applies a fortiori to the interpretations of this practice that come under the heading of the philosophy of law in our Western tradition.

Let me make it clear, at the outset, that I am very much disinclined to draw clear-cut boundary lines around either entire disciplines or subdisciplines. When writing about contemporary social and political theory in the first chapter of this book, I dealt with such theory as it is to be found in the writings of professional social scientists—that is, people who teach in social-science departments of academic institutions—as well as of professional philosophers. The division that I drew between them was more a matter of practical advantage that a reflection of ineluctable differences in principle between their respective subject matters. After all, the drawing of lines among academic disciplines always has some historical origin in a felt need for a division of labor, or sometimes simply in a dispute by two factions as to how to approach a given subject matter; in such cases, the dispute ends by one faction's leaving the original field to the other one and declaring that there now exists a new field, with a new name. So it is here with the philosophy of law, or legal theory, or jurisprudence, regarded as in some sense distinct from social and political philosophy proper. At best, the philosophy of law is a branch of social and political theory; but the expression "philosophy of law," or "legal philosophy," has come to designate an approach or a group of approaches that in some respects differs from those taken by social and political philosophers and other theorists who do not particularly interest themselves in the law.

My aim is to effect a synthesis of sorts. In chapter two I elaborated upon Sartre's contribution, as I saw it, to understanding the contemporary social and political worlds. Sartre has almost nothing to say anywhere about legal practices and institutions per se; at most, he shows that values, including legal values, and rights, which often acquire a legal form, are created within organized groups in response to the need for them to define their longer-range objectives. There is a basis here, to be sure, for his developing a more detailed account of how behavior can come about that is governed by rules that are sometimes, to varying degrees, accepted by members of *conflicting* groups within a large modern society, just as there is a basis for his giving an elaborate description of social classes and class conflicts within large modern societies. I take *both* phenomena to be real and salient features of our world: (a) the existence of legal systems whose rules are accepted [71] and abided by (though often imperfectly and grudgingly, on the part of some individuals and social groups, with a view to their eventually being overthrown and replaced by other rules) and (b) the existence of real class divisions, however much they may sometimes be muted in appearance and however ludicrously inadequate it may be to conceive of them according to a strictly bipolar model or according to some simple monetary criterion. Yet Sartre, like many other contemporary writers who have been strongly influenced by Marx, has very little to say about the former set of phenomena, the phenomena of law, and a great deal to say about the latter. (I have discussed this in detail in *Fundamental Change in Law and Society* [75].) I take this to be a serious failing on Sartre's part.

At the same time, however, as I shall show in this chapter, there is an equally serious blindness concerning all the many phenomena that surround and flow from the fact of social-class division, a blindness on the part of those who are today regarded as contributing most to the philosophy of law in our country. All that I can do here is to point to these inadequacies, to give some explanation of how they have arisen in terms of the intellectual traditions from which they have come, and to indicate how they may be related to other current social and political events. But the mere fact of doing this will, I hope, give a little impetus to new directions to be taken in social and political theory that will be less one-sided, more adequate. If I can do so at all, I shall be making a small contribution to resolving the crisis in social and political theory that we are endeavoring to explore.

What I propose to do in this chapter is first describe—initially rather impressionistically and generally, and then more specifically with reference to three writers—the paradoxical nature of the enterprise of legal philosophy, caught as it is between the philosophical demand for powerful and broad generalization, on the one hand, and the natural assumption that a legal philosophy should be rooted in actual legal practices, on the other. The three writers are, of course, the ones to whom I referred late in my first chapter, Rawls, Nozick, and Dworkin; I shall emphasize the first. Oddly enough, only Dworkin of the three writes with much background in the law itself, but all three are making an important impact on those in this country who consider themselves legal philosophers, and in any case it should be remembered that I am using the term "legal philosophy" in a very loose sense, as designating more than anything else a kind of approach to social and political phenomena.

In the second (and shorter) half of the chapter, I shall briefly review some of the factors that have led to the comparative neglect of legal philosophy within the Continental European, and particularly the Marxian, traditions of which Sartre is the heir. I shall then discuss some possible ways of using these traditions to promote a new emphasis in the philosophy of law—an emphasis that I think is already implicit in some of our textbook and journal literature on the subject, but which needs to be more fully explicated and elaborated upon than it has yet been.

The term "philosophy of law" owes its origin more to Hegel than to anyone else. This is a great paradox from a historical point of view, because by far the stronger impetus to the development of jurisprudence as a semiautonomous or even totally autonomous area within philosophy and social science has come from those who reject Hegel's rapprochement between legal institutions and their philosophical rationalizations, on the one hand, and moral and political practices and their theoretical counterparts, on the other. Hegel's *Philosophie des Rechts*, "philosophy of law," is consciously placed within the great tradition of systematic thought that goes back to Plato, to Aristotle, to Aquinas, and, closer to his own time, to Montesquieu and Rousseau. Plato's *Republic* and *Laws*, after all, are attempts to mediate between ideal justice as Plato conceives it, which for him is *real* justice, and its embodiments in the empirical world in the form of proposed legal institutions. The entire natural-law tradition had the same basic theoretical project and was premised on the notion that ideal justice and ideal rules of social and political conduct in fact coincided. This premise was reinforced by the equally close coincidence (which in fact was no coincidence at all, in the sense of a chance or accidental happening) of the words for "law" and the words for either "justice" or "right" in Latin, the Romance languages, and German—e.g., *jus* and *justitia* in Latin, *droit* for both "law" and "right" in French, *diritto* similarly in Italian, and *Recht* similarly in German, which also has the word *Gerechtigkeit* for "justice." Kant's little work on legal philosophy, which some commentators [36] have regarded as falling within the natural-law tradition, is entitled *Metaphysical Elements of Justice* [59]. Hegel was very critical, even in the early years of his career[50], of the natural-law tradition for, among other things, its retention of the idea of unchangeableness, its failure to take account of historical aspects of the development of law and of justice itself. Yet the other title of his *great* work in social and political philosophy is *Naturrecht und Staatswissenschaft im Grundrisse*—"natural law and political science in outline." So in some respects—even though the element of historical relativization that he obviously introduced into conceptions of law and justice causes some commentators to see Hegel's philosophy as a definitive break with natural-law thinking—Hegel remains within that tradition when it is regarded, as I have said, as a *systematic* linkage of the philosophical treatment of law with that of politics and morality. (On this point, see my "Marxism and Natural Law" [78].)

In the early part of his *Philosophy of Law*, Hegel shows that he is fighting on two fronts. It is obvious that he is bitterly attacking the Romantics, who believe that all law ought to be overthrown in favor of what, in *The Phenomenology of Mind*, he calls the law of the heart, or who at best disdain having to do with all existing institutions in favor of constructing a utopia, a world as they say it ought to be. Vis-à-vis these sorts of people—and here, typically, Hegel is painting with a very broad brush with a view to eliminating a great many positions all at once—Hegel appears as the hard-nosed realist, insisting that we take this world as it is. Moreover, although it is not a necessary logical consequence of such realism, Hegel additionally maintains the conservative view that the world as it is is the world as it ought to be, at least for this moment.

The second front on which Hegel is fighting is perhaps less apparent but equally important. He conducts a long polemic [54] against the growing historical school of law, and particularly against one of its representatives, Gustav von Hugo, for rejecting the philosophical treatment of law entirely in favor of straight reporting of what is to be found in the statutes. This school's researches were being conducted at that time primarily in the field of Roman law, about which a great deal was being discovered. Hegel charges Hugo with making the implicit philosophical assumption, beneath his surface hatred of philosophy, that whatever the laws at a particular time and place declared was to be taken as *eo ipso* rational. That is total conservatism, and it is not Hegel's position. What Hegel is advocating is a rational construction, or reconstruction, of the law at a given time and place with a view to finding its ideal elements; this enterprise, he believes, has become fully possible only in his own epoch and civilization. But in order to do this successfully, one must in one way or another gloss over many irrational details of the law as it is written and/or practiced. One treats such details as irrelevant to the grand scheme, and in doing so one of course criticizes them implicitly. Seen from this point of view, Hegel's position is that of a moderate reformer rather than a hidebound reactionary, even in the most conservative late years of his life. The authorities who assumed power in Prussia a few years after Hegel's death, and who by their widespread campaign of political repression succeeded in discouraging many aspiring young academics, such as Marx, from pursuing university careers, realized this about Hegel's influence and significance.

It is important to see, from a historical perspective, just who were Hegel's opponents on the intellectual Right, such as Hugo. I have indulged in this rather long excursus about Hegel in part with a view to making this point, which may at first seem surprising. It is the historical school of law on the Continent (together with the somewhat later movement inspired by the jurisprudence of John Austin, another staunch political conservative, in England) that serves as the intellectual progenitor of the modern effort to segregate the theoretical study of the law from the study of morals and politics, which goes by the name of legal positivism. (This point has been made by one of the leading historians of legal positivism, Norberto Bobbio, himself a man of the Left [22].) The slogan of legal positivism, "the law is the law," has been put forward in a number of different contexts since Hegel's day, by thinkers with quite different political orientations and motivations from those of their intellectual forebears. Legal positivism has often, for instance, been used as a weapon against natural-law thinking and against the traditional alliance between such thinking and conservative political and religious forces, particularly in the Catholic countries of Europe. But its general effect, whatever the various historical and political contexts in which it has been advanced, remains the same as it was when it first emerged as a recognizable theoretical position in Hegel's time: to emphasize the study of law as it is found empirically to exist in particular places; to place parameters around this field with a view to segregating it from other fields, such as ethics and social theory, with which it might appear to be closely bound; and hence finally to remove the existing law entirely from any possible subjection to certain forms of philosophical reflection and critique.

It is the spirit of legal positivism that has dominated, though of course not exclusively, the last hundred years of legal theory in Germany and also in the Scandinavian and Anglo-Saxon countries. It seems to me that this spirit is characterized by two apparently contradictory tendencies: first, that of taking existing legal procedures and institutions as givens, and second, that of extreme formalism. This is really quite understandable. The legal positivist begins with the intention of systematically grasping the law as it is. This means, among other things, that one is to have nothing to do with moral prejudices or with social or economic accounts of the law; the law as such is empirically given. But then, of course, one is aware that specific laws change from year to year and differ from place to place. So it would seem that what is needed is a theory of the most general features that are applicable to all existing legal systems, even though any such account is bound to be extremely formal and to gloss over the messy, day-to-day realities of the law as it is experienced by actual lawyers, judges, and citizens. When this theory has been developed, what we have must be a kind of idealization, a formal exercise. Moreover, it must be an idealization of the common features of, primarily, modern Western legal systems—European and American—because it is these systems that have determined what Western thinkers have grown up believing "the law" to be. It becomes very difficult, for instance, to fit mediational procedures—such as one finds more commonly in American Indian tribes and in certain other societies and even, increasingly, in some aspects of mainstream American social life, such as labor laws—into the formal model that one has developed; the formal model is much more apt to be based on the idea of crime and punishment, established through an adversary proceeding.

The best illustration of such an outcome is the work of the greatest of legal positivists, Hans Kelsen. His *General Theory of Law and State* [60], along with his shorter *The Pure Theory of Law* [61] and other writings, is a remarkably consistent exercise in just this sort of extreme formalization of an ideal conception of "the law" as such. It is rooted in a set of legal practices that is common to the countries of the *Code Napoléon*, the countries of Continental Western Europe, and not really to any others, not even entirely to the common-law countries of Great Britain and the United States. Kelsen totally rejects every hint of a sociological account of jurisprudence, always emphasizing the *purity* of his theory and, consequently, its scientific rigor. I think that the illusoriness of this alleged purity and rigor is a rather easy thing to demonstrate, and I attempted to do this in my article "The Essential Role of Models and Analogies in the Philosophy of Law" [73]. Still, I have great admiration for the clarity and the doggedness with which Kelsen carried the enterprise of legal positivism to its logical conclusion.

Much of the literature on the philosophy of law for the past several decades has been an amalgam of general theories about the nature of law, on the one hand, and, on the other, analyses of legal reasoning, meaning primarily the way in which judges in Western legal systems think when reaching their decisions. On the whole, if I may indulge in an outrageous generalization, the philosophy of law in Western countries has been a rather bloodless intellectual enterprise. The one movement that constituted a notable exception to this was the American movement known as legal realism, an offshoot of pragmatism and of a reaction to some particularly vacuous American legal formalisms. Unfortunately, legal realism was often less philosophically sophisticated than its positivist rivals. To say, as Oliver Wendell Holmes did, that the law is simply what the judges will decide—no more and no less—is, to start with, simply false and inadequate as a description of legal practice even in the United States, where judicial discretion is much wider than in most other legal systems. But at least the legal realists tried, in their crudely cynical ways, to establish some relationship between the law as a sort of ideal and the law as it is experienced by the various actors within it. By contrast, so much of the rest of the literature has dwelt in what the realists called "the heaven of judicial concepts" and has exuded the combined aura of the academic classroom, especially of a class in formal and informal logic, and of "the Law" in Kafka's parable. Although it has occasionally advocated reform, it has seldom suggested the need for radical reflection on, and criticism of, the system as a whole. The very way in which the standard questions have been posed—"What is the nature of Law?.," "What is the nature of Justice?," "What is the nature of judicial reasoning?"—has precluded such a more philosophically challenging approach.

Hegel's *Philosophy of Law*, with which I began this quick historical and impressionistic survey, encourages us to ask these same questions, or at least the first two; but the kind of answer it gives leaves room at least for the dialectical development of radical criticism, even though that was not Hegel's own intellectual path. The most important reason why this is so, as I have already indicated, is that Hegel's *Philosophy of Law* is simultaneously a political theory, a theory about morality, a theory about history, a theory about property and economic exchange, and so on, as well as a theory about law. Most teachers of the philosophy of law, in England and America at least, would never think of including Hegel's book in one of their courses—they would regard it as not germane to what they were interested in and as containing far too many metaphysical presuppositions instead of being empirically based. This is a very prejudiced attitude, of course, though it also contains much truth; there *is* a basic incompatibility between his approach and theirs, although it does not lie exactly where most holders of this attitude with whom I have spoken seem to think. But one distinctive feature about Hegel, whether one likes it or not, is his inclination to state his prejudices and his purposes openly. I have always been particularly struck by one passage in the preface to the *Philosophy of Right* that at once expresses the *critical* possibilities latent in Hegel's entire system of legal philosophy and the motivation that drives Hegel (and probably many other sensitive defenders of the legal status quo if they would only be willing to acknowledge it) to engage in legal and political theory in the first place:

> To recognize reason as the rose in the cross of the present and thereby to enjoy the present, this is the rational insight which reconciles us to the actual, the reconciliation which philosophy affords to those in whom there has once arisen an inner voice bidding them to comprehend,—to possess subjective freedom while standing not in anything particular and accidental but in what exists absolutely. [55]

The present is a cross, that is, a suffering, a source of pain. But the philosophical treatment of it, which is admittedly an idealization, a discovery of the rose in the cross, is a sort of therapy, a reconciliation.

I cited this passage from Hegel in a review I wrote [84] of John Rawls's book *A Theory of Justice* soon after its publication in 1971. I juxtaposed it with the last few sentences of Rawls's book, which read as follows:

> Thus to see our place in society from the perspective of this position is to see it *sub specie aeternitatis:* it is to regard the human situation not only from all social but also from all temporal points of view. The perspective of eternity is not a perspective from a certain place beyond the world, nor the point of view of a transcendent being; rather it is a certain form of thought and feeling that rational persons can adopt within the world. And having done so, they can, whatever their generation, bring together into one scheme all individual perspectives and arrive together at regulative principles that can be affirmed by everyone as he lives by them, each from his own standpoint. Purity of heart, if one could attain it, would be to see clearly and to act with grace and self-command from this point of view. [125]

It struck me at the time I wrote the review, and it still strikes me, that there is a considerable resemblance between the two passages—that both affirm the idea of philosophy as consolation and resolution of antagonisms. This is not a bad motivation for doing philosophy—it is a recommendation, in fact—as long as it does not somehow blind us to the realities of the actual world that we are studying. In other words, the desirability or undesirability of this standpoint depends on the ontological status that one assigns to it. In Plato's thought, for instance, although the world of the Forms is said to be the truly real world, a tension is maintained between that world and the one in which we live at present; in Neoplatonism there is a clear retreat from this latter world—in part a reaction, no doubt, to the changed political situation of the Hellenistic period. The case of Hegel is more complex in this respect than is that of Plato, because a standpoint of transcendence is attainable for Hegel only by virtue of our being the outcome of a long historical process; human history counted very little for Plato. Rawls, in *A Theory of Justice*, says that he is not really trying to set down an epistemology or an ontology at any length, and in the passage that I have quoted he explicitly rules out the cruder forms of Platonistic interpretation that could be placed on his notion of a position *sub specie aeternitatis*—that is, the idea that the position is situated in a space "beyond the world," or that it is the standpoint of some transcendent being. Nevertheless, I think that the passage furnishes a very important insight into Rawls's entire project and its cultural and theoretical significance.

Rawls's work is worth some attention here for several related reasons. It received tremendous recognition, as philosophy books go, when it first appeared, just eight years ago. Most students of Rawls have heard, for instance, of Stuart Hampshire's claim, in his review in *The New York Review of Books* [48], that it is the most important work of postwar Anglo-American moral philosophy. It has already been the object of a remarkable number of studies—book-length examinations by Brian Barry [15] and Robert Paul Wolff [176], an anthology of essays edited by Norman Daniels [31], a full section of the *American Political Science Review* [4], and others. I first taught it as part of a summer political-theory course at Northwestern University in 1972, and since then it has undoubtedly been one of the readings—often the exclusive reading—in hundreds of courses and seminars in political philosophy, ethics, and in the philosophy of law. The result of this close scrutiny has, of course, not been a consensus that the book is flawless; Rawls himself never claimed any such thing. To begin with, he readily admits that the third major part of the book, entitled "Ends," which has to do with the Rawlsian conception of goodness as it relates to justice, is unfinished, sketchy. It was simply that Rawls did not wish to wait any longer before having the book published; the book was already nearly six hundred pages long.

This leads us to another aspect of the Rawls phenomenon as a cultural event: His book had been long awaited by numerous American philosophers. Preliminary essays that were eventually incorporated (though often in drastically altered form) into the book date back more than a decade prior to its publication; the first and best known, entitled "Justice As Fairness," was first printed in 1958[123]. The study of justice had been Rawls's lifework as a researcher; although he is still not "aging," it seemed to be time, in 1971, to set down some of his conclusions in a systematic way.

There is much to admire about Rawls's work. It is very careful, it tries hard not to be dogmatic, it makes numerous references to other writings in philosophy and economics, and its thesis is one that, if implemented, would lead to our living in a society that in many respects would be more humane than the contemporary American one. Rather than a sycophantic adulation of current American social and political institutions, in other words, it is mildly critical. This is reassuring to me, since I believe that social and political theory, when it is truly philosophical, must always contain at least some element of criticism.

Having admitted all this, however, I think it safe to say that *A Theory of Justice* rather clearly suffers from what I have been claiming about the majority of literature in the philosophy of law: that it tends at once both to excessive generality and to excessive specificity—limitedness to a relatively narrow social and cultural perspective—in a way that raises fundamental doubts. *A Theory of Justice* does not, in fact, rely at all heavily on recent literature in the philosophy of law. H. L. A. Hart, for instance, who before the publication of Rawls's book was unquestionably the best-known writer in this area in postwar Anglo-American philosophy, receives mention in only thirteen footnotes; this is not a great deal compared with the total number of footnotes in the book. What is more important, Hart nowhere receives a sustained examination by Rawls. Kelsen is never mentioned. But, as I have already said, the fact that Rawls's central concern is justice has been sufficient to cause most legal philosophers to adopt him as one of their own. Moreoever, he does have something to say about specifically legal issues, such as civil disobedience and conscientious refusal, discussed in his sixth chapter. Nevertheless, whatever may be the subcategory of philosophy within which one classifies Rawls's book, the fact remains that it fits into the pattern of excessive generality and excessive specificity that I have noted before. It does not, in other words, take very seriously the notions either of historical change or of significant cross-cultural differences.

I shall quickly summarize the main points of the book, then list a few of the innumerable internal criticisms that have been raised by myself and others, and finally attempt to place the book in a cultural perspective; from this perspective it will be possible to go on to consider the books by Nozick and Dworkin in less detail. Once again, as with Sartre's *Critique*, I shall assume no detailed knowledge on the part of my readers.

Most of the heart of Rawls's position is developed in his first few chapters. His methodology consists essentially of a mental process that he calls reflective equilibrium, whereby one scouts some of the various institutional arrangements that have been proposed by different philosophical camps as best fulfilling the ideal of justice, and then one balances these alternatives and makes appropriate adjustments in one's mind until a conception of justice is achieved that is most consonant with one's best, most unprejudiced intuitions on the subject. It is taken for granted, from the outset, that justice is our highest social ideal and hence most worthy of being delineated in this fashion. Rawls proposes that we try to imagine a society of individuals who are in the most unbiased possible situation in which to decide, by common and universal agreement, just which principles should be adopted as standards for justice for themselves, their families, and their immediate descendants. This abstract, hypothetical situation—which resembles the old Lockean notion of the state of nature but without any admixture of empirical, historical fact such as we find in Locke and others—is called "the original position" by Rawls. The occupants of the original position are then covered with a "veil of ignorance," meaning, essentially, that they are to know nothing of what their particular statuses will be within the society whose rules of justice they are to draw up. In fact, their ignorance is to be very great; as Rawls says,

> It is assumed, then, that the parties do not know certain kinds of particular facts. First of all, no one knows his place in society, his class position or social status; nor does he know his fortune in the distribution of natural assets and abilities, his intelligence and strength, and the like. Nor, again, does anyone know his conception of the good,* the particulars of his rational plan of life, or even the special features of his psychology such as his aversion to risk or liability to optimism or pessimism. More than this, I assume that the parties do not know the particular circumstances of their own society. That is, they do not know its economic or political situation, or the level of civilization and culture it has been able to achieve. [126]

On the other hand, however, these imaginary parties do know the following:

> It is taken for granted . . . that they know the general facts about human society. They understand political affairs and the principles of economic theory; they know the basis of social organization and the laws of human psychology. Indeed, the parties are presumed to know whatever general facts affect the choice of the principles of justice. There are no limitations on general information, that is, on general laws and theories, since conceptions of justice must be adjusted to the characteristics of the systems of social cooperation which they are to regulate, and there is no reason to rule out these facts. [127]

When placed in this position, Rawls asserts, the parties would choose the following two principles as fundamental:

First Principle:
    Each person is to have an equal right to the most extensive total system of equal basic liberties compatible with a similar system of liberty for all.

---

*For Rawls, although the conception of justice must be universal, conceptions of the good both do and ought to differ from one individual to the next.

Second Principle:
Social and economic inequalities are to be arranged so that they are both:
(a) to the greatest benefit of the least advantaged, consistent with the just saving principle,* and
(b) attached to offices and positions open to all under conditions of fair equality of opportunity. [128]

And this, to paraphrase Thomas Aquinas in his proofs of God's existence, is what all men call justice.

We need to consider certain explanations of what the two principles entail and the reason for the second one, called "the difference principle," to which Rawls devotes far more attention. Rawls, of course, devotes many pages to such elucidation, but I can only try to single out a few highlights. First of all, these two principles are supposed to be lexically ordered— that is, in cases in which the full enforcement of the one interferes with the full enforcement of the other, the first principle, that of liberty, is to be given priority over the second, the difference principle. Rawls makes one exception to this, and it is the only concession in his book, as far as I can see, to the relevance of historical change to social theory: He admits that the lexical priority of the liberty principle may not be able to be sustained in a society at a very primitive, low level of economic development.

The next point of elucidation has to do with the things that count for Rawls as needing to be arranged—or "distributed," to use the economic term that is never far from his mind—in accordance with the difference principle. These "things" turn out to be what he calls "primary social goods." His first listing of them consists of the following broad categories: "rights and liberties, opportunities and powers, income and wealth" [129]. He then adds that much later in the book he will introduce an important new primary good, namely, a sense of one's own worth. To paraphrase Rawls, then, justice in the distribution of such "goods" consists in not allowing it to be unequal unless, and then only to the extent to which, an unequal distribtuion can be shown to be of greater benefit to the member of society who is least advantaged in terms of these goods, than the benefit that this same member would receive if total equality of

---

*This has to do with making provision for the needs of future generations.

distribution prevailed. Rawls has little doubt that as a rule inequality can be shown to be more beneficial than absolute equality both to the least advantaged and, probably, to most of the rest of society; but his idea of a just society is one in which the extent or amount of inequalities would be sharply limited by the difference principle, probably more limited than is the case in the United States today. This is the point at which Rawls's theory has a critical thrust.

Another notion Rawls elucidates is "fair equality of opportunity." He distinguishes it sharply from the notion of "equality as careers open to talents." "There is no more reason," he says, "to permit the distribution of income and wealth to be settled by the distribution of natural assets than by historical and social fortune." [130] In this respect, then, Rawls is an extreme egalitarian.

Finally, Rawls bases his claim that these are the principles of justice that the parties in the original position would choose on a notion taken from game theory called the maximin rule for choice under uncertainty. As he says, "The maximin rule tells us to rank alternatives by the worst possible outcomes: we are to adopt the alternative the worst outcome of which is superior to the worst outcomes of the others." [131] Rawls reasons that the parties in the original position would not know which place they would individually occupy in the society that they are setting up, and so, in accordance with the maximin rule, they would shun principles sanctioning greater inequality, since any one of them might end up at the bottom. In connection with this I should mention one final restriction that Rawls places on parties in the original position, a restriction that contrasts with what we think of as characteristic of human beings: The parties in the original position are incapable of the emotion of *envy*.

The remainder of the book, once the principles have been laid out, deals, first, with the imagined implementation of the principles in political and economic institutions through the device of a constitutional convention, and, second, with the relationship between justice and goodness. Rawls admits the possibility that his principles of justice would be compatible with a market socialist economy, but not with any nonmarket form of socialism. On the whole, however, he seems to think it more probable that a modified version of capitalism would obtain in a Rawlsian state. He continues throughout the work to establish a distance between his philosophical position and utilitarianism, and his criticisms of various versions of the latter constitute some of the most trenchant chapters in *A Theory of Justice*. Let us now, for the sake of brevity, turn to some of the difficulties of the theory that strike me as most important.

Many readers are bothered, and I think rightly so, by the way in which Rawls has structured his argument for his two principles. The abstractness of the concept of the original position, the sense in which it is deliberately presented as a thought experiment, an academic exercise with no possible chance of being even partially simulated in the real world, causes one to have many doubts about the appropriateness of the device. This criticism raises a very complex set of issues. Every social theorist engages in one form or another of abstraction from reality—singling out certain general features and neglecting certain specific idiosyncracies. But not every form of abstraction is equally legitimate and/or informative. It should be pointed out that Rawls's procedure is modeled on a combination of the traditional state-of-nature idea taken from early modern political philosophy (but purified of some of the historical residues for which these thinkers have been most seriously criticized) and a type of thinking that is common among economic theorists. If this appeal to past and present authority is taken as a vindication of Rawls's general procedure, then so be it. But there are at least three features of the details of Rawls's account that seem especially questionable. One, to me the most devastating, is the distinction Rawls makes in the long passages concerning the "veil of ignorance" between the particular facts of which the members of the original position are forced to be ignorant and the general facts that they are permitted to know. There is much about what Rawls calls "general facts" that is taken to be general only among people who accept, as I for one do not, certain paradigms of mainstream contemporary American social science as universal truths—paradigms about psychology, politics, economic theory, and even what Rawls calls "the basis of social organization." [127] But it is precisely because none of these matters are the clear-cut, indubitable facts that Rawls thinks them that books like Sartre's *Critique of Dialectical Reason* have a purpose and a potential value!

Another feature of Rawls's account of the original position

that has raised many hackles is his decision not to allow the parties in this position to experience envy. The decision does, of course, remove a potentially distortive element from them while they are making up their minds, but there seems to be something particularly arbitrary about this move. Can we say that these parties (who, strictly speaking, are not individuals, but representatives of several generations of families, since otherwise there would be nothing to stop them from deciding to use up all the earth's resources during their own lifetimes) are really human?

A third feature that has come in for criticism from some of the economists and games theorists themselves, such as Kenneth Arrow [10], is Rawls's assumption of the maximin rule. There are many cases of ordinary experience in which almost no one would act on a maximin basis. For example, there is the choice I have between traveling home from Pittsburgh to Indiana, in which case there is a slight but statistically real possibility of my being in an accident, and not traveling home. (Actually, a more compelling example is the choice of whether to go to Pittsburgh from my home in the first place, since in the case of the return trip I would have to balance out the serious disadvantages of not going.)

Other points on which Rawls has been sharply criticized, from a variety of political and disciplinary perspectives, include his egalitarian rejection of talent as a basis for preference in society (this is one of the few important points on which I agree with Robert Nozick), his very basic assumption that all normal people would agree, more or less, with his list of primary goods, and his extremely inadequate defense of the equal right to liberty. On this last point, it is not that I disagree with him on the importance of freedom as a human social end, but that I find most unacceptable his easy rejection of the notion that there is some intimate and not merely accidental relation between the claim that one is free and the claim that one has the wherewithal, the real and not merely theoretical capacity, to act freely. It is important to note what Rawls has to say— and this is just about all he has to say about it in the entire book—on this matter:

> A final point. The inability to take advantage of one's rights and opportunities as a result of poverty and igno-

rance, and a lack of means generally, is sometimes counted among the constraints definitive of liberty. I shall not, however, say this, but rather I shall think of these things as affecting the worth of liberty, the value to individuals of the rights that the first principle defines. [132]

Many other readers besides myself have found this treatment very inadequate.

Let me now withdraw from the text of *A Theory of Justice* in order to look at the book as both a product of its times and a certain definer of trends in philosophy and in the broader culture. It is a gentle book—very much the opposite in tone of Sartre's strident and violence-filled *Critique*. It is, as I have already mentioned, very consciously reminiscent of that product of the best of leisurely Victorian thinking, Sidgwick's *Methods of Ethics*, even though philosophically Rawls cannot support even the very modified form of utilitarianism at which Sidgwick arrives. It is painstaking in its own way; Rawls has a talent for anticipating objections—which is not so surprising when one realizes that much of the prepublication text was seen and commented upon by some of the best philosophical minds in America.

But that, to me, makes it all the more distressing that the gaps in Rawls's book are so very large. He simply has not taken account of (and I do not mean "agreed with," only "taken account of") radical alternative views about justice, such as the Marxian view that theories of justice are parts of the dominant ideology, or situationist views, or indeed any views that assign one or another form of historical relativity to the concept of justice. He accepts unquestioningly the theoretical framework of contemporary bourgeois economic theory, not only on economic issues, such as its disallowance of non-market forms of socialism as worthy of consideration, but even the psychological and ethical aspects of such theory; the theory assumes one or another version of universal egotism and then derives all its conclusions about what would be chosen on the basis of this assumption. (Remember that Rawls's entire theoretical structure is an argument to the effect that this is what rational parties in the original position *would choose* as their principles of justice, and what they would choose is determinative of what justice is.) Economics determines the very sort of answer that Rawls decides to seek: essentially, the justice that he is looking for is a justice of distribution of goods.

When it comes to defining how the parties in the original position should be conceived, Rawls suggests that we think of them as fathers of families. In this and in one or two other remarks, he shows that he has no desire to take account of alternative conceptions of the family structure—as, for instance, Plato did so brilliantly and so controversially in the *Republic*. Again, I am not saying that Rawls should have advocated the replacement of the nuclear family with something else—simply that he should not have *assumed* the existence of the nuclear family in the way that he does. He also assumes, though in this case he at least acknowledges that it is an assumption, the existence of a world of nation-states more or less as we have it at present. He has stipulated that he is concerned with justice at the level of social institutions, so that in a sense he can excuse himself for not dealing with international justice, on the grounds that no significant institutions exist at the international level. But the point is that today so many of the most salient questions about justice and injustice are being raised, by both theorists and political leaders around the world, at just this level: The world's unequal distribution of food, fuel, and other scarce and dwindling resources is a matter of the utmost concern, and it is increasingly being regarded as a matter of justice.

I could elaborate much further on the lacunae in *Rawls's* vision, but I trust that my point is now clear: His entire approach, though enormously detailed at times, is somehow both narrowly Western, or even Anglo-American, and yet also "above it all." It is permeated with the same paradox of excessive specificity and excessive generality with which I have charged the whole recent tradition of philosophy of law.

Moreover, the appearance of rigor in Rawls's book is somewhat misleading. It is detailed, yes. But at crucial points, beginning with his discussion of reflective equilibrium right at the outset, Rawls makes a heavy appeal to what he calls our "intuitions" on the subject of justice. And he does not mean "intuition" in a Husserlian or Cartesian sense! Ever since *A Theory of Justice* appeared, I have heard more and more moral arguments conducted in terms of pitting one discussant's "intuitions" against another's. And, while perhaps this is preferable to ethical arguments premised on the belief that we can resolve all the substantive issues by reducing our terms to logical symbols, it is equally unhelpful to the cause of real rigor and seriousness.

100

Finally, Rawls's book seems to have answered a real felt need of the time at which it was published. Granted, it was many years in preparation, and when he began it Rawls could hardly have anticipated all the tumultuous events that took place in the intervening years. A hint, though very slight, of those events crept into his discussions here and there, notably in his chapter on conscientious refusal. But *A Theory of Justice* reached publication at a time when those events—the civil-rights movement and the protest against the Vietnam draft—were beginning to fade into memory. Many charges had been made during that period to the effect that our institutions were unjust. People wanted to know, perhaps more than they did just prior to the 1960s, what justice was, anyway. Rawls told us. He told us that it was not merely an emotive utterance, as some of the philosophers of the early 1950s would have done. He suggested that ours was not a perfectly just society, to be sure, but that, on the other hand, we were not so far off the track. And, without abandoning social concern, Rawls advocated a reflective stance that brought purity of heart, at a time when there was much talk of turning inward and rediscovering one's psyche. One may develop whatever views of causal connection or else, alternatively, of accident that one wishes about these coincidences that I have noted, but the important point is that *A Theory of Justice* fitted in well with its zeitgeist.

We have considered what Rawls has told us about himself and also, briefly, what he has told us about our society. What about the other two writers to be treated here, Robert Nozick and Ronald Dworkin? Their books *Anarchy, State, and Utopia* and *Taking Rights Seriously*, respectively, are very disparate works; to compare them is to compare apples and oranges. But both make considerable reference to Rawls, and both also say a great deal about our society and, hence, ourselves.

If Rawls's book corresponded well with certain trends of the early 1970s, Nozick's picks up on other trends that became more noticeable in the middle of this decade, when his book appeared (1974). If Rawls is always moderate and balanced, Nozick tries, it seems, never to be so. The key to his thesis is "entitlements." This means, essentially, property rights, if one uses property in the Lockean sense, of life, liberty, and estate. For Nozick, entitlements are and of right ought to be unequal, and the purpose of government is to protect them, and nothing more. He attempts to show that the effort to do so outside of and prior to a formal state would lead to the formation of mutual protective agencies, giant insurance companies, which would gradually merge and eventually come to resemble the minimal state that he is advocating. Thus, anarchism is, to his mind, refuted. But any state activity beyond this minimal level is unacceptable, because it would violate one's entitlements. Utopia in the sense of a single coherent blueprint for society is a wicked, wholesale violation of entitlements; the only acceptable sense of utopia is a state of affairs in which everyone makes the most profitable use of his (Nozick is not prone to say "his or her") entitlements.

Nozick occasionally shares with us some very interesting side arguments and discussions; one of the best known is his argument for the plausibility of the notion of animal rights, which came at a time of rising interest in this topic. He also includes some detailed criticisms of Rawls, who is Nozick's colleague in the Harvard philosophy department. But on the whole, it is neither a well-written nor a well-argued book. Many besides myself have read it in surprise that a publisher would allow it to appear in such very rough form. Nozick defends, and indeed takes pride in, this roughness, on the grounds that his readers are thus sharing in an ongoing process of thinking—he calls it "exploration" [111] with him. As for the argument, after two readings I have failed to find a sustained defense of the philosophical basis for the key concept of entitlements. It is assumed, and the argument moves on from there. But the book has received, after all, national recognition and awards. Would it sound too absurdly sinister and silly if I said that there are some powerful interests who would like to see Nozick's message succeed through advertising? I hope not.

In any case, what I find most distinctive about Nozick's work is the *passion* one finds in it. Nozick is a very passionate man in the cause that he serves. He was, as I understand it, a participant in some of the student protests of the 1960s. In one way, he gave up all that; his alliance is now with the Right and not the Left. But in another way, he did not. There was a very banal slogan that had its origins in one segment of the sixties protesters—those who stood for the counterculture and against the tedious theorizing and civic-mindedness (albeit civic-mindedness of a radical or even revolutionary type) that one found among the Marxist-influenced and other socialist segments. The slogan was "Do your own thing." Hegel had satirized it a century and a half earlier in his *Phenomenology* as the spiritual kingdom (or community) of animals [51]. I do not care much where Nozick personally stood in the spectrum of the student protest movement. What I do believe is that he has provided us, in his book, with a very sustained and philosophically informed defense of the message contained in that slogan.

Nozick does not advocate coercion; far from it. He wants authorities to be minimal about it, in keeping with the aim of protecting property. But he consciously dismisses all the real coercions that exist and are systematically imposed if one is a holder of very few or no entitlements in a society in which a great many of them are floating around. If Rawls's *Theory of Justice* seems for the most part to ignore the contradictions and agonies that confront people daily in our present legal and political system, Nozick's book seems to find no difficulty in accepting, as an essential part of social existence, all contradictions except those that result from non-minimal-state activity. It treats life like an entrepreneurial challenge. As for individuals or whole societies that are underprivileged, it seems to be saying, "Tough muffin!"

This, at least, is my hasty and no doubt somewhat over-drawn overview of Nozick's social philosophy. Between it and Rawls's theory, it is difficult to decide which is further from social reality. Rawls is at times ethereal; Nozick is not, if one thinks of the ether as being tranquil. Nozick is somewhat less provincial than Rawls in his philosophical references, and in place of Rawls's obvious reference to American historical models in such devices as his constitutional convention, we have Nozick's protective agencies. Nozick is much more of a social critic, albeit a critic from the Right, than Rawls is. But in Nozick, too, I find a strong cultural bias; he seems to be saying that his is a rigorous and consistent version of basic Lockean—and thus, by inheritance, American—liberalism, and hence to be calling for a return to these roots and an abandonment of the Great Society type of social endeavors of the 1960s. Need I remark that there are many, many politically weary individuals, from philosophers to ordinary citizens to presidents, in

103

whom this approach strikes a sensitive chord today? And once again, far more blatantly than in Rawls, *economics* is said to have the implements to furnish us with a cure.

Dworkin's essays, collected under the title *Taking Rights Seriously*, span about a decade; the book was published in 1977. The work is far more philosophically and culturally provincial than either Rawls's or Nozick's. Dworkin gives very little evidence of knowing much in depth about the history of either philosophy or legal theory, with the exception of the work of his former mentor and predecessor in the Regius Professorship of Jurisprudence at Oxford, H. L. A. Hart. Moreover, the argument that Dworkin makes for his thesis that preconceptions about rights underlie lawyers' and judges' reasonings can be based only on the American and, to a limited degree, British legal systems (he admits that the situation in Great Britain is rather different because of that country's lack of a written constitution). Dworkin uses this thesis philosophically to undermine legal positivism in general and its Hartian version in particular. Hart at one point claims that where clear-cut legal rules are lacking for judges to decide a case, the judges must then engage in an activity resembling an imaginary game called "Scorer's Discretion" [49]. Dworkin contends that there are standards and principles, not just positivistic rules, in the law, and that these are what judges do and should rely on in baffling circumstances. He also uses his thesis about the fundamental nature of rights to supply, as he sees it, a missing undergirding to Rawls's account of the "original position" and the choice of just principles. It is interesting and, I think, not chargeable to absolutely pure coincidence that Dworkin's book came upon the philosophical scene at the height of President Carter's campaign about human rights. One of the criticisms that was frequently made about this campaign was that it implied an assumption of moral superiority on the part of the United States compared with other countries, a denial that there were any beams in our eyes that needed to be removed. Whether or not this was entirely fair to Mr. Carter—and I do not really think it was—the criticism of a certain condescending tone about rights certainly applies to Dworkin's writings.

And yet, having said all this by way of fairly severe criticism of Dworkin, I must confess that I find something very much to admire, something of real positive value, about his work. He has taken to heart Bentham's, and many others', criticisms of the formal notion of a right conceived as a kind of spiritual part of a person, analogous to an arm or a leg, though not Bentham's conclusion that the whole concept is therefore nonsensical. He admits that rights claims must sometimes yield to considerations of policy, and that there is no miraculous formula for determining when this should be. He sees the legal life-world, in other words, in a far less formalistic, far more realistic way than did most of his predecessors in the tradition of legal philosophy. In Dworkin's approach, there lies some hope.

Moreover, Dworkin has confronted and tried to come to grips with real problems. When, at the height of agitation over the Vietnam draft, the Solicitor General of the United States, Erwin Griswold, delivered a speech at Tulane University in which he declared that all violators (however conscientious) of the law against counseling draft resisters should be prosecuted, because not to do so would make a travesty of the law, Dworkin wrote an essay showing that this hard-line stance was consonant neither with his own thesis about rights nor with long-standing American constitutional and legal traditions. This essay appears in *Taking Rights Seriously [40]*. Writing for *The New York Review of Books* and traveling in interesting circles both in this country and in England, Dworkin perhaps embodied the image of "radical chic," at the time when that expression was current, as much as anyone. But that is not necessarily such a bad thing. If a careful reading of his essays shows him, in retrospect, not to have been very radical at all, at least he seems to have shared some of the concerns and goals of more truly radical thinkers. Perhaps he opens up some possibility of rapprochement.

With this as my cue, I would like to consider a peculiarity of most radical political thinkers, among whom I include Sartre and contemporary Marxists, in the Continental European philosophical traditions: namely, their failure to pay much attention in their work to rights or other law-oriented phenomena.

Marx regarded terms such as *right* and *justice* to be specific to the social mode of production in which they were being used. That is, he had observed the ideological use to which they were constantly being put by writers defending the existing

105

system—capitalism in his day, but feudalism or what have you at another time—and for the most part he eschewed their use in his writings. It is very paradoxical: Here is a writer who is obviously tremendously concerned about the issues of social morality that are usually grouped around the concept of justice, and yet that concept plays almost no role in his thought. Yes, he and Engels say in *The Communist Manifesto*, we communists want to overthrow bourgeois right and bourgeois justice, because these ideas function in defense of a class structure that is fundamentally . . . what? Unjust and wrong? Well, they do speak a great deal of "exploitation." But the way in which they use that word is such that it is definable strictly in descriptive, even quantitatively descriptive, terms. The rate of surplus value in a productive industry for them—s/v, surplus value over variable capital—is also called the rate of exploitation. The two terms are equivalent.

There is one rare, very interesting passage in *Capital* [97] in which Marx discusses the wage-contract relationship between a capitalist and a worker in terms of whether or not it is an injustice. It is fundamentally equal, of course: The worker has been forced to sell his or her labor to the employer, and he or she has had no choice in the matter. To the worker, Marx implies, it appears as a trick. But is it unjust? No, as long as there is actually no fraud in the legal sense involved, since the legal system that reinforces the existing economic arrangements has defined the wage contract as a relationship of strict *legal* equality between capitalist and worker, and hence as right and just.

A philosophical literature, to which I myself have contributed an article, [72, 1, 43, 108, 169, 178] has sprung up around this passage and a few others in Marx's writings on the topic of justice. I tend to endorse Marx's great reluctance to use such words as *right* and *justice* to designate social relationships in what he calls a society of associated producers, which he envisages for a possible future postcapitalist era. Marx deliberately says very little about that future society, but I think that he sees words such as *justice* and *injustice* as disappearing from use in such a society, since they will no longer have any referents, except in the study of previous social forms.

However, there are difficulties with Marx's position, and as usual it is Engels, the popularizer of the doctrine, who sometimes fails to grasp subtleties, who reveals the difficulties to us by "going overboard." In one section of his essay "On the Housing Question" [41], Engels claims that justice is a totally relativistic term—relative, that is, to its usage by every individual. Moreover, he analogizes it to phlogiston, that supposed chemical substance that eighteenth-century scientists thought to be the basis of combustion, but which was then, of course, found not to exist.

Without taking the time to puzzle over this for too long, since Engels is not our primary concern, I can state without hesitation that there is something wrong with Engels's way of putting it. He and Marx need to have, as I have just shown they do have, a theory *about* justice that is applicable to different individuals and different societies in order to be able to make the claims that they do about the ideological function of the term justice. This suggests that, while it is strictly incorrect for someone who agrees, as I do, with basic aspects of Marx's (and others') critique of traditional justice-talk to speak of a theory *of justice*, it is acceptable to speak of a theory *about* justice, injustice, and wrong. And indeed, emphasis should rightly be placed on the plural forms of the latter two terms, injustice and wrong (paradoxical as this may sound in light of the mainstream tradition of Western social philosophy, of which Rawls is the contemporary heir). I suggest this because actual injustices and wrongs in two senses—(a) discrepancies between prevailing legal ideals and actual practices and (b) blatant exploitations that are *sanctioned* by prevailing ideals—do exist in the everyday world. In contrast, justice as such exists nowhere, not even in the print on the six hundred pages of John Rawls's book.

I am reminded of a passage in Thomas Hobbes on the subject of the so-called summum bonum; the parallel between it and our present subject is not exact, but it is worth citing anyway:

> For there is no such *finis ultimus*, utmost aim, nor *summum bonum*, greatest good, as is spoken of in the books of the old moral philosophers. . . . Felicity is a continual progress of the desire from one object to another, the attaining of the former being still but the way to the latter. [56]

If we now turn from Marx and speak about other, more contemporary representatives of Continental European philosophy, we find, as I have already noted, that they have very little to say about law, right, and justice. Of course *some* European thinkers have a great deal to say about these subjects—the Belgian Chaim Perelman [113], for instance, or the Dane Alf Ross [134], but that is precisely because these individuals have rejected mainstream Continental thought in favor of what they can find in the tradition of Anglo-American legal philosophy or in other disciplines. Moreover, my generalization requires some further qualification. Sartre, for instance, is rather fascinated by the notion of *rights;* in the *Critique of Dialectical Reason* he shows how the pledge that is taken by members of a fused group in order to ensure its permanence creates all kinds of mutual rights and duties. But elsewhere in this book, and certainly in his other writings, he shows that he thinks of *rights* primarily in the sense of the philosophically arbitrary and unfounded claim made by possessors of privilege and power that they *deserve* that privilege and power, whether by divine gift, or by birth, or simply by some asserted excellence.

This sense of *rights,* it seems to me, is fairly close to Nozick's use of *entitlements.* Sartre once wrote a very fine short story that conveys this meaning well. It is called "Childhood of a Leader" [138] and tells the story of a young man born into a well-to-do family who as a university student becomes a member of a rabid right-wing group that goes around beating up Jews; unfortunately, we sometimes forget that such phenomena were widespread in France as well as in Germany in the 1930s. This future leader is constantly insisting on his "rights." The same characteristic obtains in the cases of the bourgeois "bastards" (*salauds*) whose portraits are hung in the Bouville art gallery in Sartre's novel *Nausea.* To me, Sartre's description [151] of Roquentin's visit to the portrait gallery of the founding fathers of modern Bouville is one of the most unforgettable in literature. These founding fathers had been suffused with a sense of *droit*—right and law, the two English words having the same equivalent in French, were on their side. My point is that most of the connotations of the word for Sartre are clearly negative.

Merleau-Ponty has a number of reflections to make about law and justice in his book *Humanism and Terror,* but they are about Soviet law and Soviet justice, as manifested in the Moscow purge trials of the 1930s. And it is really the implicit *ethic* of the judges and prosecutors (who, in these cases, were members of the same team), rather than their legal practices, that is of interest to him. What he does not take note of in this work, and what might have been helpful for him to mention (or even for Arthur Koestler to mention, since it was his novel *Darkness at Noon* that furnished part of the inspiration for Merleau-Ponty), is that the period when these trials began was the very period that wrote *finis* to the most promising and brilliantly original single national outpouring of legal theory in our century and perhaps *any* century, Soviet legal theory of the 1920s.

M. A. Reysner and E. B. Pashukanis were two of the greatest names of this movement, but there were many others, who are anthologized in Babb's massive volume [14]. The movement had its origins, of course, like the Bolshevik movement itself, in prerevolutionary Russia. These theorists were deeply concerned with the paradoxes of maintaining a legal system in a country where both the state and its legal system were supposedly withering away, and they were also concerned with the practical issues of how the legal system should be redesigned to serve the new society and how the revolutionary Soviet government should act in relation to a system of international law that was dominated by bourgeois states. These were all tremendously important issues, and they seemed to be real enough in the heady atmosphere of experimentation and newness that characterized life in the U.S.S.R., despite all external and internal threats, in the early 1920s. But the writers in question need not have bothered grappling with the issues, it seems. By the early 1930s Stalin was in control and was proclaiming the strengthening, as opposed to withering away, of the Soviet state. His principal legal theorist, who officially declared Pashukanis and the others to be wrongheaded and dangerous, was none other than Andrei Vychinsky, who became the chief state prosecutor at the Moscow trials and later, after World War II, the principal Soviet delegate to the United Nations for some years. This whole history, which is more forgotten than remembered even by those who should realize its significance, sheds a great deal of light on the peculiarity to which I am pointing, namely, the disregard of legal theory and concepts on the part of mainstream Continental European philosophy.

Was what happened in the Soviet Union all due to the terrible aberration known as Stalinism? I am afraid not. The record will show that the intellectual way to the suppression of the school of Soviet legal philosophy was prepared by the thought of Lenin, particularly in his famous work *State and Revolution*. Lenin believed he was being faithful to Marx, and perhaps he was. I only want to stress one point (which I have analyzed in more detail elsewhere [81]) from that book in respect to the phenomenon of law. It is this: For Lenin, there can never in *any* sense be a state governed by laws, a *Rechtsstaat*. For, according to him, *Recht* (law) is opposed to *Diktat* (decree), and the ruling class in capitalist and precapitalist societies always governs in its own interest by a dictatorship over the masses. Even when you have a proletarian revolution, until the state withers away in the distant future you have a dictatorship of the proletariat. So there never has been, and never will be, a state of law in any sense; such a notion is for Lenin a bit like phlogiston.

A very similar idea is expressed in a 1920s essay by the great Hungarian philosopher György Lukács. Entitled "Legality and Illegality," the essay is contained in his famous book *History and Class-Consciousness* [69]. The piece is certainly not Lukács at his most profound, but that does not matter for present purposes. His point is to warn against both taking the defenders of bourgeois law at their word about the sanctity of the legal system, and making a fetish of counterlegal violence. But the bourgeois state and its legal system ultimately *are* violent, for Lukács, and at this level of analysis he and Lenin agree.

That is all very well as far as it goes, but the fact remains that the phenomena of bourgeois law exist. By "phenomena of bourgeois law" I mean the practices of millions of ordinary citizens, not just officials, in Western capitalist and other countries, in which the legal system is *accepted* as somehow legitimate as it controls large areas of their lives. This is not, let me repeat, analogous to the acceptance of phlogiston by eighteenth-century chemists. The Marxist theorists may be correct— I think that they are—in asserting that there is a great deal of illusion making or mystification involved in theorizing that these legal systems are imperfect but reasonably successful approximations of pure, blind, neutral, interest-free justice. But then there is a need to explain those practices whereby the law is made to *appear* unprejudiced in many areas of its operation, so that those who do not belong to the dominant social classes will believe that it *is* somewhat unprejudiced. In the actual working out of the law, in other words, we by definition do not and cannot remain at the level of *mere* appearance, *mere* illusion. And this is a point that most Marxist theorists have not faced.

I should mention, in passing, one who has tried to face it, Nicos Poulantzas. He has done so from a rather hard-line, neo-Althusserian, Marxist-Leninist position, which makes his achievement all the more remarkable. His trilogy—*Political Power and Social Classes* [122], *Fascism and Dictatorship* [121], and *Classes in Contemporary Capitalism* [120]—is not easy to read, but, as I have pointed out in a critical review [85], it opens up a number of new vistas.

Poulantzas's second title, *Fascism and Dictatorship*, reminds us of one final, very important reason for the neglect of law by mainstream Continental philosophy. It is the still recent and overwhelming experience of Nazism and other forms of fascism, which was so much more keenly, because personally, felt on the Continent than in England or the United States. What Nazism taught, above all, was the possibility of *manipulating* the *Rechtsstaat* in the interests of a fascist dictatorship. In Germany, the historical process was very simple: The Weimar Republic had provision for the declaration, at a time of emergency, of a "state of exception." At the time of the *Reichstag* fire in Berlin (which now seems to have been set by the Nazis), Hitler succeeded in having such a state of exception declared; the political mood was one of hysteria. By virtue of this step, Hitler's emergency decrees, which thereafter continued to be issued until the collapse of his regime, achieved a certain gloss of legality, even though they eventually overthrew all the democratic practices and protection of private rights that had existed under the Weimar constitution. In other words, a good case could be made for the contention that, from a formal, constitutional point of view, the Nazi regime had legitimacy; indeed, it was this sort of argument, coupled often with a self-serving belief that things would be even worse if they resigned, that led many German judges and officials of the legal system who were not enamored of the fascist ideology to stay on in their positions. (Of course, there were plenty of judges and lawyers who wholeheartedly *supported* Nazism, too, but that is another story.)

This whole experience—which was repeated with some variation in France when the Vichy regime surrendered its powers to the Nazi occupation at the start of World War II—could only engender tremendous cynicism about the claims of the law as a pure guardian and promoter of justice. Kafka was a prophet; the world of law in Continental Europe, East and West, throughout much of this century has been Kafka's world. It is going on that way today in his native city of Prague, and it has been going on that way again, to a much greater extent than most Americans realize or want to admit, in Germany, in its recent atmosphere of terrorism and counterterrorism. How can the claims of the defenders of the law's purity be taken seriously under such conditions? And why should Continental philosophers take seriously the ideas that seem to exercise solemn but politically innocent Anglo-Saxons such as Dworkin and Rawls?

That, in a nutshell, is the current situation in the philosophy of law in relation to other aspects of social theory, as I see it. For very good historical and political reasons, as well as for reasons related to the different intellectual traditions that accompany the political differences, there exists a vast gap between two universes of discourse on legal theory, and there has been very little attempt to bridge it. I can put it more concretely in terms of personal experience. When, in 1971, I went from Korčula, Yugoslavia, where I was a staff member in the Korčula summer school on social and political philosophy, to Brussels, Belgium, where I participated in the International Congress on the Philosophy of Law, it was indeed a trip from one world to another, far more than the overnight boat and plane and train trip would lead one to expect. The Korčula meeting included many of the Yugoslavian *Praxis* philosophers and Jürgen Habermas and others who were thoroughly steeped in Marx and Hegel and Heidegger and Sartre, whereas the Brussels meeting was dominated by American, British, and Australian legal philosophers primarily from the positivist tradtion. The two groups seemed to be discussing two entirely disparate sets of phenomena.

What, as Lenin would say, is to be done? I do not think that it is hopeless, or I would not be writing about the problem and thereby trying to bridge the gap myself. It seems to me that certain trends in current legal philosophy as it is taught and thought about in our country *may* in fact be conducive—I emphasize the word *may*—to a rejoining of the two traditions and the development of a sounder, more realistic, and, from an explanatory point of view, more adequate legal philosophy than what we have had in the recent past.

Let me recall, first of all, what I wrote earlier about Ronald Dworkin's work: it is naive and provincial in its perspectives, both on the history of philosophy in general and on the history of legal theory in particular, but at least it speaks to some concrete issues. What it speaks to, or at least one way of putting what it speaks to, is perceptions, common to Dworkin and his audience, of "injustices and wrongs" in the way the law is administered. Many such perceived injustices and wrongs have their basis in socioeconomic inequalities—for example, the administration of the draft laws during the war against Vietnam tended to favor those economically advantaged over the disadvantaged, and the thorny issue of discrimination and so-called reverse discrimination, to which Dworkin also addresses himself, is of course tied in large measure to historical inequalities in income between blacks and whites and females and males. Dworkin says very little about the broader social implications of such facts; it would be expecting too much if we thought he would elaborate on this. Nevertheless, he does talk about these injustices and wrongs and how philosophically they ought to be adjudicated. He writes in a way that is intelligible to lawyers and judges and even the general educated public; perhaps that is partly because many of these essays were written for *The New York Review of Books*. The quasi-popular character of Dworkin's work is all to the good: our philosophy, especially our legal philosophy, needs desperately to break out of the limits of narrow professionalism.

Meanwhile, certain trends—about which I shall be writing at greater length in chapter four—are abetting philosophy in doing just that. Enrollments in traditional academic courses in philosophy are declining; the pressures on students are severe to take only what is deemed practical, and philosophy is usually *not* deemed so. But the philosophy of law is a good candidate for being considered an exception. After all, the law is experienced by everyone, and used at some time or another by most. And since most professional philosophers today make their livings as professors, they realize that to fail to develop courses that more students will attend means the end of professionalism entirely! So the wise plan of action seems to be to promote courses such as those in the philosophy of law.

The type of student who enters a philosophy course out of the pragmatic motivation just described is not very likely to respond well to the traditional questions legal philosophers raise—"What is law?," "What is justice?," and so forth. This student has been conditioned, by long training guided by the presuppositions of our culture, to expect a course entitled "Philosophy of Law" to provide him or her with instructions in the workings of Plato's great, strong beast. On the other hand, a philosopher cannot in conscience, if he or she is to be faithful to the discipline's purpose of raising critical questions, simply offer a course in legal mechanics—or legal husbandry, if we stick with the Platonic imagery. How to resolve these divergent expectations? Here we find, in a concrete, practical, now common situation, one aspect of social theory at a crossroads.

The outlines of a resolution, which of course is easier to describe than to bring about, consist in referring to the fact that the law is experienced, often enough, as a sequence of "injustices and wrongs"—the very phenomena concentrated on by Marx and Engels and the whole recent tradition of mainstream Continental theory, even though these words are not usually employed. Such an emphasis is useful not just in the obvious case of the innocent citizen harassed by government officials—perhaps by wiretapping—or of the victim of a frame-up. Nor does this notion even apply simply to the class of poorest citizens (roughly speaking, Marxism's "proletariat"), who statistically receive far severer sentences than citizens of other socioeconomic groups for crimes of a similar magnitude. The notion that the law is frequently experienced as injustices and wrongs applies also to the *victim* of crime in our society, who may easily be a middle-class citizen suffused with "respectability." The recent literature of legal theory is filled with a new awareness of the law's going very hard on a victim who presses charges or cooperates with the authorities in doing so. The amount of time, effort, lawyers' fees, and sheer frustration involved doubles or triples the deprivation caused by the original criminal act. The most notorious type of crime in which this occurs is, of course, rape. But this rule also applies to accident victims, burglary victims, and others. So injustices and wrongs are a more commonplace experience within the functioning of the law than we are prone to acknowledge.

If one approaches the philosophy of law topically, in this way, a great many of the deformations that have plagued traditional legal philosophy as I have described it have a much smaller chance of developing. In this approach one is certainly apt to avoid the idea that there is an all-embracing form of law or of injustice, applicable to all times and places, as well as the excessive formalism and generalization that result from holding to this idea. I have deliberately spoken of injustices and wrongs: the danger of excessive specificity is still present in the topical approach, but it is no greater than in the traditional approach, with the latter's tendency to draw all examples and problems from British and American law. Moreover, the new emphasis increases the *possibility* of avoiding narrow Anglo-American legal provincialism. For students and teachers alike are apt to be more familiar with ways in which legal systems other than their own generate, or at least encourage, the perpetration of injustices and wrongs than they are with how the courts or other judicial institutions in those systems actually function. For instance, when speaking about the knotty problems surrounding insanity and the law, one can parallel the Soviet practice of declaring dissidents insane and sentencing them to mental institutions (surrogate prisons) with certain similar practices developing in American law. In sum, the possibilities of a less provincial legal theory than we have had up to now do exist, and the approach I am sketching may facilitate their realization.

Textbooks that employ this new approach are beginning to be developed; there is one, for example, edited by my former colleague Kenneth Kipnis [62], that exemplifies the approach quite well. The danger, of course, is that textbooks of this kind could be mere pap, written at a low, journalistic level and without the editors' or authors' bringing to bear any sense of the rich philosophical tradition that, whatever its flaws, is there to be tapped. For what needs to be done, and indeed *can* be done, by a teacher or writer employing this approach is to lead

115

students and readers from a consideration of the specific to a consideration of the broader issues. This has always been the preferred method of philosophers, but it has sometimes been forgotten, when writers—often motivated by the ideological need to present the law as the kind of glowing, unapproachable presence of Kafka's parable—have *begun* by speaking in vast generalities about the nature of law and justice.

We can assume very little cultural background in many of our students today. That state of affairs is to be the starting point of my final chapter. But we can make a virtue of this adverse situation by leading them from their mutual experience of the law as it functions to a comprehension of it as an ingredient in our social and economic structures, an ingredient bearing no real resemblance at all to the law of Kafka's parable.

CHAPTER FOUR

Socio-economic Bases of the Current Crisis in Our Culture

I use *culture* in the broadest possible sense. It refers to both the life of the universities and the pursuits of those who are not connected with universities, to both "high" and "popular" arts, and to technology, as well—in short, to all those achievements of our society that distinguish it from past societies in terms of patterns of behavior, institutions, and ideals. To put it another way, *culture* is going to be used here in anything but a technical sense. By "our" culture, I mean primarily American, secondarily Western European, and finally, the global cultures that American and Western European cultures have played a role in defining.

I maintain that our culture is in crisis, that the crisis in social and political theory that we are dedicated to exploring is simply an aspect of this crisis, and that social theory, if it is rightly conceived, should make the explanation and proposed resolution of this crisis its principal task.

Crisis is a much overworked word, and perhaps I could have found a less trite one. I have no intention of entering into the usual speculations as to when the current crisis in culture began, whether this crisis is the worst one ever, and so on. Perhaps, however, my use of *crisis* has a greater value now than it would have had five or ten years ago, because others are now speaking less of crisis, yet the reality of crisis seems greater now than then. A decade ago, the war in Vietnam was very much on everyone's mind, there were protests verging on, and sometimes becoming, riots, and there was much talk of something called a counterculture. Now, by contrast, all is relatively calm; we have peace, nearly no one protests anything, and most people cannot even remember what the idea of counterculture was all about.

Indeed, the loss of historical memory is one of the principal features of the crisis. Ours is a society geared to the present, and perhaps in some measure (though in declining measure, if recent polls are to be believed) to the future. But the past is something that by and large is not regarded as important to know about. Of course, we have our revivals of period moods—our Victorian revival, our twenties and fifties and now even our sixties revivals. These movements have commercial possibilities, and so they are exploited. But real historical knowledge, knowledge of origins, is generally discounted. As evidence of this, consider the very inferior role that the study of history plays, not only in the undergraduate curriculum of today, but even in the training of professionals, future professors, in the humanities and the social sciences. The typical doctoral program in, for example, psychology or sociology includes few or no requirements that students learn the history of their own disciplines; this of course reflects the self-understanding of these disciplines as empirical descriptions of contemporary behavior patterns or institutional structures, treated as if they were eternally true and therefore eternally valid. Even in philosophy, the rejection of history, as having little importance, is more the rule than the exception. Some of the founders of the analytic movement in philosophy, such as Gilbert Ryle, were persons of considerable culture, as we often express it, meaning that they were knowledgeable about the past as the background to the present; but the philosophical emphasis that they fostered resulted in a sharp decline in historical knowledge on the part of the majority of the succeeding generations of philosophers within that tradition, since such knowledge seemed to be of little value for the new conception of philosophy. Wittgenstein, as it has now become a platitude to point out, read his classics more or less on the sly. At its outset even the phenomenological tradition of Continental philosophy entailed a certain rejection of history. Husserl, its founder, was not very well educated in the history of philosophy when he began his researches, and little knowledge of history is required in order to follow his *Logical Investigations*. Later on, of course, he wrote at length about the *Crisis of European Sciences;* in order to understand the nature of the crisis one must comprehend, as he came to, the historical factors that have entered into its constitution. With Heidegger's insight into the nature of the metaphysical tradition of Western thought, on the one hand, and French phenomenology, with its integration of the Husserlian method with the broad dialectical tradition of Hegel and Marx, on the other, modern phenomenology came to acquire a very firm sense of history; but it is a minority current among the academic disciplines and methods in our culture today.

It is indeed true that ours is a mass culture, which cannot be defined exclusively in terms of what happens among small groups of intellectuals or professional academics. I might remark that those two categories can certainly not be considered synonymous or coextensive in our culture; one of the points I have been making can be put another way by saying that a great many academic disciplines today do not encourage intellectuality, but rather only the development of skills supposedly required to understand Plato's "great, strong beast." In a number of past societies, it is often said, there were two rather clearly distinguishable cultures, one of the elite and the other of the folk, although since the preservation of the latter culture was generally not through writing, as was that of the former, our knowledge of past folk cultures tends to be sparse. In any event, in our society this sharp distinction is said to have become blurred, which I think, with some qualifications, is correct. But if it is true that what is in the mass media is more indicative of the nature of our mass culture than what is going on in academic circles, my point about the decline of historical memory in our society becomes even starker and more forceful. Anyone who is in the habit of watching television will realize what I mean.

Today our mass-circulation magazines, whenever they do refer back to the 1960s, more often than not refer to them as a time of iconoclasm, when students deserted their studies en masse and flocked to the banner of Jerry Rubin and other charlatans who attacked our social and cultural institutions out of no more serious motivation than the desire, perhaps, for self-aggrandizing publicity. I have heard many colleagues in philosophy repeat this lament about the recent past. But Jerry Rubin and the Yippies were very much a minority in the ferment of the 1960s, seized upon fervently by the mass media because simple iconoclasm was easier to comprehend than intellectually disciplined radical protest. They made such good copy.

119

My memory of the 1960s is rather different from the dominant negative image that is in circulation today. It was, of course, a time of great upheaval, often very upsetting. But the root cause of the upheaval, at least in the second half of the decade, was the American government's escalation of its war against Vietnam. This should be an obvious point, but it is now often forgotten. It was also a time when philosophy courses were far more popular, compared with the present, than were, let us say, accounting courses. Was this because philosophy professors were seeking to be "relevant," in the superficial sense of the word, wearing beads, maybe smoking some "pot," and generally leading the iconoclast assault? In some highly visible instances, yes: but that was not the main reason for philosophy's popularity. To put it in a nutshell, the study, the *serious* study, of philosophy had a central significance for the students of the 1960s that it does not occupy now because philosophy appeared to be one academic discipline that did not quite fit the model of the study of the "great, strong beast," and its practitioners, even when striving to conform to the rules of "the Establishment," always seemed to fail to do so.

Perhaps we can understand a little better just how this ambivalence in philosophy's self-image played its role in the culture of the 1960s—in fact, in an international culture, not just our own American culture—if we consider the case of one very prominent philosopher of the period, Herbert Marcuse, and his best-known book of the same period, *One-Dimensional Man* [94]. If, as I hope, parts of this final chapter can be taken as a contribution to a critique of contemporary culture, *One-Dimensional Man* is one of a relatively small number of books that seem to me to serve as more or less worthy models of this sort of philosophical endeavor. I realize that for some a look back at Marcuse may elicit any one or a combination of several negative emotions, such as embarrassment, boredom, or contempt. Embarrassment could be the reaction especially of those who took Marcuse and his work seriously at the time, and now wonder why they did. Is it possible that this German Hegel scholar—who when he was still teaching at Brandeis University in the late 1950s and early '60s was not deemed suitable company, so to speak, for the members of the philosophy department, but instead was employed as a political scientist and intellectual historian—should at one point in the late 1960s have been selected *president* of the Pacific Division of the American Philosophical Association? I am sure that many a member of the A.P.A. would today find that a very bewildering fact; at best, he or she could understand the election as a political statement of the time, which of course it was, but nowadays it is difficult for many to understand the meaning of a political statement.

In any case, Marcuse's work was very much studied in the 1960s—primarily, to be sure, at an undergraduate level, but that implies that graduate students and faculty members also studied it in order to use it in their courses—and the man's fame spread rapidly. I might contrast two personal encounters that I had with him—the first in January 1964, the very month *One-Dimensional Man* was published, when I arranged for him to speak to the Graduate Philosophy Club at Yale on the topic of his critique of analytic philosophy in that book, and the second in November or early December 1968, when the Yale philosophy department, of which I was then a member, invited him to be its final speaker in a lecture series on revolution. If statistics about quantity ever have a significance beyond mere numbers, here is a clear-cut instance of it. The 1964 meeting was attended by about twenty or twenty-five persons (as the principal arranger at the time, I kept note of such things). I was not disappointed by that attendance, although of course I would have liked to see more. At the 1968 session, one of the largest halls in the university was filled far beyond capacity a half hour before the talk began, even though it was also being broadcast on the university radio station. At that time, Marcuse's audiences everywhere were similar in size. One has good reason to be skeptical about cultural phenomena that (or, as in this case, who) become fads. I saw Professor Marcuse after his lecture, later that evening, surrounded by adulating students in an atmosphere in which a discussion of issues was obviously no longer possible. He had been counterfinalized by events; he was obviously very uncomfortable, but also very much gratified by the extent to which, as it seemed, his critical message was finally being taken seriously—I repeat, *as it seemed.* Was it, in fact, or was this just an illusion? An interesting speculative question.

What, then, was Marcuse's message in *One-Dimensional Man?* Let me begin by putting it in the context of his earlier works. His great study of Hegel, primarily of Hegel's *Phenomenology*, written before Marcuse was exiled from Germany by the Nazi onslaught, was called *Reason and Revolution* [95]; it purported to show the possibilities for radically critical thought that were latent in Hegel's philosophy and indeed in the dialectical method itself. *Eros and Civilization* [93] was an internal critique of Freud's philosophy, attempting to show that, although Freud had concluded that the maintenance of civilization required a suppression and bridling of libidinal energies, the hard rule of *anankē*, this would not necessarily obtain in a society in which scarcity had been overcome. In such a society, for Marcuse, what Freud called the pleasure principle could be allowed full play without endangering the achievements of civilization and occasioning a relapse into barbarism. Finally, Marcuse's book entitled *Soviet Marxism* [96] attempted to argue that the very existence of blatant contradictions between the repressive and bureaucratic actuality of present-day Soviet society and the liberating elements of the theory, including the idea of the withering away of the state, to which the Soviet government was still officially committed, left some room for hope for that country's future.

One-Dimensional Man is a flawed book, of course, perhaps more seriously flawed than any of the other three just mentioned. Probably the most obvious flaw has to do with the historical negation of the book's major premise soon after its publication. The premise is that our society is one in which even the consideration of radically alternative structures to the present ones has been closed off by the manipulation of language in the communications media, in industry, in the social sciences, and in philosophy. True, Marcuse holds out a slight possibility of breaking through this one-dimensionality at the very end of his book, but it is *extremely* slight. This is what he says:

> However, underneath the conservative popular base is the substratum of the outcasts and outsiders, the exploited and persecuted of other races and other colors, the unemployed and the unemployable. They exist outside the democratic process; their life is the most immediate and the most real need for ending intolerable conditions and institutions. Thus their opposition is revolutionary even if their consciousness is not. Their opposition

hits the system from without and is therefore not deflected by the system; it is an elementary force which violates the rules of the game and, in doing so, reveals it as a rigged game. When they get together and go out into the streets, without arms, without protection, in order to ask for the most primitive civil rights, they know that they face dogs, stones, and bombs, jail, concentration camps, even death. Their force is behind every political demonstration for the victims of law and order. The fact that they start refusing to play the game may be the fact which marks the beginning of the end of a period.

Nothing indicates that it will be a good end. The economic and technical capabilities of the established societies are sufficiently vast to allow for adjustments and concessions to the underdog, and their armed forces sufficiently trained and equipped to take care of emergency situations. However, the spectre is there again, inside and outside the frontiers of the advanced societies. The facile historical parallel with the barbarians threatening the empire of civilization prejudges the issue; the second period of barbarism may well be the continued empire of civilization itself. But the chance is that, in this period, the historical extremes may meet again: the most advanced consciousness of humanity and its most exploited force. It is nothing but a chance. The critical theory of society possesses no concepts which could bridge the gap between the present and its future; holding no promise and showing no success, it remains negative. Thus it wants to remain loyal to those who, without hope, have given and give their life to the Great Refusal.

At the beginning of the fascist era, Walter Benjamin wrote:

"Nur um der Hoffnungslosen willen ist uns die Hoffnung gegeben."

It is only for the sake of those without hope that hope is given to us. [94a]

Yet, within a few months, a serious protest movement had developed, and it was not just within the outcast and fringe elements of society that it manifested itself. The very success of Marcuse's book, one might say, belied its principal premise. But now, a decade and a half later, we have reason to wonder whether this belying of the premise was not a very temporary phenomenon, and whether the one-dimensionality of our society that Marcuse discerned is not, after all, still its most salient feature.

Another flaw, clearly, in Marcuse's account is his treatment of analytic philosophy. He strongly criticizes it for its alleged assumption that ordinary language, as it is spoken at a particular place and time, is normative, since this assumption, of course, eliminates all possibility of advocating linguistic reform. But his criticism applies strictly to at best only a small group within the broad movement of analytic thought, and perhaps even to that group for only a limited period of time. Still, Marcuse was able to find some citations that gave his contention considerable plausibility.

He can be faulted in a similar manner for being too broad-brushed in his critical portrayal of operationalism in the social sciences. But when all is said and done, I think that the positive value of *One-Dimensional Man* still outweighs its flaws. Marcuse could blend the findings of popular sociologists of the late 1950s—such as Vance Packard, author of *The Hidden Persuaders*, and William Whyte, author of *The Organization Man*—with a rather complex and extremely interesting historical analysis, one of the best I know of, of the meaning of dialectics, in a way that makes sense of both. I think this illustrates the appropriate way to do philosophy in an era of mass culture, even if Marcuse himself was not always successful in carrying out the project. Although I know there are colleagues who would disagree with me, I believe that the insistence on a certain purity in one's philosophizing, in which one avoids all contamination by other disciplines, mistakes the very nature of philosophy and leads to its death. Such an attitude definitely leads to the death of social and political philosophy.

Thus Marcuse's *One-Dimensional Man* epitomized a particular spirit both inside and outside of professional philosophy during the 1960s. Of course the book was damned by many and ignored by many more, but still it reinforced the notion that philosophy, as least in the dialectical form advanced by Marcuse, provides an Archimedean point for radical social criticism.

If, as I believe, philosophy still performs that function, the fact is not very well known or much thought about, and if and to the extent it is known, it is regarded by much of our society as a mark *against* philosophy rather than in its favor. For we are, indeed, in a period of something like what Marx called a "slaveholder's revolt," a period when strong reactionary forces are abroad, striving to make certain that "the lid is on" all over society. And this attitude of making certain no protest is heard is applauded by many persons in academic life with at least as much enthusiasm as it is by political authorities—sometimes even more. Why this is so has a great deal to do with the pressures under which academicians live, pressures generated from socioeconomic conditions. But before I enter into a consideration of these conditions, I shall attempt to draw up a general statement of some of the other major features of our contemporary culture, features in addition to the loss of historical memory that occasioned this excursus back into our recent past, the 1960s.

A second obvious feature is our culture's spirit of self-indulgence or hedonism, epitomized in the book title *Looking Out for Number One*, which recently dominated the best-seller lists. As long as I am mentioning popular readings of our culture, I should also refer to the many works selling so well concerning the achievement of better sexual experience; they, too, of course, fall under the same general rubric of self-indulgence or hedonism. But this particular form of hedonism, as I conceive it, is a rather joyless thing: looking out for number one has become a serious task, a full-time occupation. One is constantly being reminded of the danger of falling behind in the self-indulgence race.

And this leads directly to a third feature, to which I have already referred, a characteristic that has tremendously important implications for those of us in academic life today. It is the tendency of so much of our society to insist on pursuing only what is deemed "practical." Granted, there has always been a strong current of this sort in American life, but it seemed for a time in the 1960s that it might be undergoing some modification. Now, on the contrary, the current seems stronger than ever. We philosophers ask, or *should* ask, immediately upon hearing someone stress the pursuit of the "practical," "Practical *for what?*." But in our society at large, people believe that this question does not need to be asked, that we all know what is meant by "practical," and it is something quite positive. "Practical" in the vernacular of our culture means that which will conduce to "getting ahead," to promoting the interests of oneself, or at most, one's immediate family. Again, as philosophers we ought to react by asking what is meant by one's "interests"; Plato was among the first to show the ambiguity of this familiar way of speaking, and a whole series of philosophers, including Marx and, at least by implication, even the great pragmatist John Dewey, have followed in his footsteps. But in the mainstream of our culture, it is regarded as obvious what constitutes one's "interests," namely, the maximizing of one's private pleasures, which in turn is thought to be achievable only by the accumulation of as much wealth as possible.

The ramifications of this attitude in academic and intellectual life are clear. If a certain academic subject or reading cannot be shown to conduce directly to the goals that I have specified, then that subject or reading is deemed a waste of time. If college can be shown, as some recent statistics would have it, to be of only marginal utility in terms of projected future income, then one ought to consider whether or not to waste one's time going to college. University job-placement officers are quoted repeatedly as saying that the humanities are a waste of time; "the jobs just aren't there." Frequently, they mention no other standard, no other possible reason for pursuing an area of study; in my experience such notions as intellectual worth are almost *never* mentioned by these individuals.

Beneath these features of our culture, and many more that I could cite—such as the appalling sexism that has continued and to some extent even increased, despite the brave efforts made in the early to mid-1970s to eliminate it—there lies one phenomenon that seems to me even more pervasive than all the rest. It is what I would like to call "the dominance of the economic." By this I mean that it is economic criteria that are used, more than any other sort, to determine what should survive and what should be allowed to perish, and that the concept of *economic* value remains, within our society, the fundamental form of value. In other words, we still live—perhaps more completely even than did our forebears in the mid-nineteenth century—in a society dominated by Marx's "fetishism of commodities." I shall now elaborate on what this claim means for the study of social and political theory, and in doing so I shall of course refer extensively to Marx and the Marxist tradition, since it was Marx and his tradition that first developed this approach in a systematic fashion. I shall then discuss the application of this approach to contemporary developments within our culture, and particularly to the current condition of academic philosophy.

Many philosophers find the Marxist approach uncongenial, because of its emphasis on economic factors. Marx himself is often dismissed as a proponent of something called "economic determinism," as though it were obvious (a) what that means, (b) that Marx held it, and (c) that it is clearly wrong. It seems to me that Marx cannot be held, on the basis of the systematic examination of *Capital* and his other important writings, to endorse the view that we can predict the future of existing socio-economic structures with any degree of certainty; hence, if that is what is meant by economic determinism it is not Marx's position. I have tried to show this in some detail in my book *The Philosophy of Marx* [82], and I do not want to go over that ground here. What I think really bothers a great many philosophers about Marx, and accounts for the superficial way in which some of them dismiss him as an "economic determinist," is his apparent abandonment, after the earliest years of his career, of philosophy in favor of economic analysis. There does seem to be considerable warrant for regarding him in this way. For one thing, he admits, in the preface to his *A Contribution to the Critique of Political Economy*, to having settled accounts with his former philosophical conscience in writing *The German Ideology* and thenceforth (that is, after 1846) turning to the study of political economy. Moreover, long sections of *Capital* are devoid of any explicit references to philosophical issues; some of them are as gray and dismal in their recounting of the factual details of how the capitalist system operates (I am thinking especially of most of volume two) as any of the works of the political economists to whom Marx was supposedly opposed.

But to see *Capital* and Marx's other mature work in this light is to disregard the fundamentally philosophical, social critical *purpose* that continued to be Marx's aim in these writings. His early analyses had gradually led him to see that the economic structures of society operate at a deeper level, so to speak, than the religious or even the political structures that had first occupied his attention. We can see him beginning to reach this conclusion even in his very early *Critique of Hegel's Philosophy of Right*, in which Marx comes to perceive that the economic domain that Hegel called "Civil Society," and to which Hegel assigned an inferior and supporting position vis-à-vis the organs of the state itself, could be shown, through a combination of internal critique and reference to actual conditions, to be the raison d'être of the modern state. We can see this insight developing in Marx's *1844 Manuscripts,* particularly in "Private Property and Communism" and in the extremely powerful, though very brief, section on money, with its references to Shakespeare's *Timon of Athens.*

Now, Marx was a perfectionist, a bit of an intellectual fanatic in the sense of wanting to pursue every line of research to its bitter end, no matter how many months or years that might take. So his subsequent commitment to detailed economic research and theory was simply the lifelong carrying out of a research direction that was imposed upon him by his early philosophical inquiries. If this project altered the history of philosophy and shattered for all those thousands of later philosophers the old idealistic self-image of philosophy as the pure pursuit of pure ideas in every domain, in abstraction from the mundane facts of the actual social world, that was indeed the purpose behind the research. Marx himself, however, never managed to pursue his project to the end or anything close to it. His projected treatment of the state, for instance, was never written, for he had not gotten nearly that far in his analysis by the time he died; in fact, he had only just *begun,* as I mentioned earlier, to take up the phenomenon of social classes, which had to be dealt with prior to that of the state.

But let us always remember, when we are thinking of Marx and the Marxist tradition in respect to the dominance of the economic, that Marx perceives and analyzes such dominance, which he finds to be characteristic of our modern society, with a view to establishing the real possibility of *overcoming* such dominance in a future society of associated producers. That is the whole *point* of Marx's lifework! Thus, the critical perspective from which Marx writes is not *itself* one of acceptance of the dominance of the economic as inevitable and eternal.

Here I wish to make an important aside, which will serve to link some of my concerns in this chapter with the discussion in chapter three of our contemporary legal philosophers. John Rawls, by contrast with Marx, really does accept the eternal dominance of the economic in his scheme of eternal justice. It is not just that Rawls is fascinated by contemporary economic theory, as he undoubtedly is (though more as an outsider to it than an insider). Beyond that, he thinks of his justice as a distributive scheme, a distribution of shares. To prove my point beyond the shadow of a doubt, I need only recall that what he calls "the principles of economic theory" [126] are among those items that the parties in his "original position," who are supposed to be kept ignorant of the exact period in history in which they will be living, are nevertheless supposed to know. So Rawls stands very clearly on the side of those who believe that basic economic principles are eternal, in the sense that they obtain across different historical periods and different societies, whereas Marx stands clearly on the opposite side. Robert Nozick, too, holds Rawls's prejudice about the dominance of the economic, but in a much cruder and less sophisticated way than Rawls does.

A little earlier I referred to Marx's expression "the fetishism of commodities" as a good one for characterizing an important feature of our contemporary culture, a feature that I, as did Marx in his time, take as a keystone for all the rest. This expression is the title of an early subsection of *Capital*, one that has been the subject of some controversy. Those who see Marx as having changed his position radically from his earlier to his later years consider the discussion of commodity fetishism in *Capital* an unfortunate reversion. But I think that that is a minority opinion; most people see it for what it is, a brilliant excursus in which Marx clearly shows the sense in which the concept of *alienation*, which had loomed so prominently in his earlier works, is the key, when understood in the particular form that it assumes within capitalism, to all that he is doing there. In order bettter to draw a contrast, he explicitly discusses [98] the kind of alienation that he considers characteristic of medieval society, and of course he also makes implicit reference to the forms of religious alienation typical of primitive fetishist societies. As far as the Middle Ages are concerned, Marx is able to show the linkage between the religious beliefs and practices and the economic conditions of feudalism. But he does not insist, because it is not part of his purpose to do so, that the economic sphere dominated medieval life in anything like the sense in which it dominates the modern world. What he stresses, in fact, is the important paradox that economic relationships of inequality were far more open during the Middle Ages than now—everyone could see who was lord and who was serf and what their respective powers were—whereas the key to the modern contractual relationship between capitalist and laborer is that both are assumed to be equally free in formal, legal terms, while beneath the surface the one holds, so to speak, all the trump cards in the relationship. Marx shows that the fetishism of commodities plays a far more determinative role in a world in which religious and other more person-oriented relationships have been unsentimentally swept away by capitalism's onslaught.

Thus throughout *Capital* and the other works of Marx's mature years, the underlying, presupposed theme is the critical one that I have been stating concerning the dominance of the economic in capitalist society, together with the possibility of society's eventually transcending this state of affairs. I shall offer just one explicit conceptual illustration of this latter aspect of Marx's insight, the possibility of going beyond the whole structure of present-day society. It has to do with a notion that plays an important and generally positive role in Marx's thought, that of *productivity*.

Marx emphasized productivity both with respect to capitalist society and with respect to a future socialist society, which, as I have noted several times, he calls a society of associated producers. This fact *might* be taken to imply that Marx is himself dominated by economic thinking in just the way that I accuse Rawls of being, because *productivity* is a term on which contemporary Western economists rely a great deal. But the interesting thing about Marx is that he conceives of *productivity* in two quite different ways, depending on whether it is being applied to capitalist or to postcapitalist society. In the former case, he accepts Adam Smith's definition of *productivity* as meaning, essentially, work for profit. Occasionally, in fact, as Marx shows in his long work *Theories of Surplus Value* [103], Smith conceived of productivity in a crudely materialistic sense, meaning the making of physical goods, but of course that would rule out, among other things, the idea of a productive— "profit-making"—*service*. Generally, however, Smith meant by *productive* whatever activity generates profit, and usually when Marx is critically analyzing the capitalist system he adopts, in his usual way, the terminology of the system whose internal critique he is providing. But there are passages in which Marx makes it clear that productivity in a much broader, unalienating, more human sense would become possible for the first time in postcapitalist society. Under postcapitalist conditions such intellectual activities as developing social theories and writing books would not be judged productive only if they made a profit for the trustees of a university or for a publishing house, but instead would be considered productive simply as expressions of their producers, the authors. The same would obtain, of course, for various manual activities, such as crafts, which now do not really "count" in our society as productive unless they generate a profit. This idea of productivity, then, provides just one interesting illustration of the way in which Marx presupposed and manifests the idea of the future overcoming of the dominance of the economic, which for him is the salient feature of modern society.

How did Marx arrive at this central insight? It can only have been through a technique of examining the structures of everyday life in his society that was, in a very meaningful sense, "phenomenological." In the preface to *Capital* he expresses concern lest his systematic presentation of the features of the capitalist system appear too "perfect," too cut-and-dried, to be realistic. And he speaks there of a method of inquiry that had to precede the method of presentation but which is not reproduced in the volume itself. It is this method of inquiry that I regard (as I have shown elsewhere [79]) as the phenomenological moment of Marx's work. Several modern followers of Marx—among others, Agnes Heller, Karel Kosík, Henri Lefebvre, to some extent even Gajo Petrović—have taken up, in one form or another, this idea of a critique of everyday life. And it is through the process of this phenomenological critique that we can come to see our society, our culture, as being dominated by commodity fetishism.

What are the specific structures that Marx discerns through his inquiry? I shall not go into detail, but shall point out the general form of his results, since this bears on the question of the Marxist approach to the discussion and explanation of cultural phenomena that is the object of the present analysis. Basically, Marx claims to have discerned a level of social reality that lies beneath the surface appearances of daily life, a level he calls the "sphere of production." What occurs in this sphere is taken to be explanatory of the forms of human intercourse that are found on the surface. It is at the depth level, the sphere of production, that the capitalist extraction of surplus value from human labor occurs. The systematically based need for the capitalist to maximize surplus value and perpetually to expand and accumulate more capital, or run the risk of going under, constitutes a rudimentary account of how the system works, on the basis of which all the rest follows. Back at the surface, this systematic necessity is expressed as the drive for maximizing profits and, within certain social and legal and technical constraints, of minimizing wages.

This brings us back to the central issue of this chapter, that is, whether such an approach can be employed to shed light on the crisis of our culture, and if so just what sort of light. In *Capital*, at least, Marx usually mentions such matters in brief asides. He refers, for instance, to the impact of capitalism on family life [99]: it has broken down old patterns, by forcing all family members to work to maintain subsistence, but this has at the same time paved the way for newer forms of human relationships. He refers also to education, and here he perceives the impact to be complex: At a certain stage of industrial development some skills are required, and hence a certain technical education must be provided. At the mass-production stage, however, there is no longer a need for any training in skills. But this very elimination of the need for technical training may well lead, with the introduction of radically different social structures, to the development of well-rounded individuals [100]; here Marx was being very optimistic. In still another cultural area, Marx refers on several occasions to the absorption of scientific research, which until that time had managed to maintain a semiautonomy, into the capitalist orbit, in that it would thenceforth be forced to place itself increasingly at the service of capitalist enterprise; here he was highly prophetic. Then, of course, Marx makes numerous references, in still another cultural domain, to the people he calls "vulgar economists," the unworthy, highly ideological successors of Adam Smith and David Ricardo—people such as Nassau Senior, who had bitterly opposed the British Ten Hours Bill (which limited labor to that daily maximum) on the ground that it was from the final hour of work, between the tenth and the eleventh or the eleventh and twelfth, that manufacturers reaped all their profits [101].

So Marx does make numerous, though brief, references to ways in which the systematic machinery of capitalism that he has described contributes to, and hence explains, aspects of the culture in which he was living. However, this application of his economic analysis was not his principal theoretical objective, at least not in what he succeeded in writing throughout the later years of his life. Consequently, his legacy in this area consists of an approach, a pointing of the way, rather than a definitive statement. And this, as far as I am concerned, is just as well, since many details of the Western cultural landscape have altered a great deal since Marx's time, and so a critique of our culture based, in a very loose and undogmatic way, on his approach would in any case need to be undertaken anew.

A few comments on two kinds of cultural phenomena that Marx's approach helps us understand are in order before I apply the approach to specific aspects of our contemporary crisis. First, the approach enables us to understand better why certain types of human activities wax and others wane or become suppressed within our culture, on the basis of the perceived centrality of the contribution that they make or fail to make to our complex modern system of commodity exchange, rather than on the basis of their value for human existence. For instance, Marx's approach enables us to comprehend the present decline in liberal education, which is considered comparatively irrelevant for the preparation of persons suitable for work in the more technologically advanced areas of contemporary culture, and might even prove counterproductive if it gives them "strange" ideas. The same approach enables us to understand why services such as health and transportation—which if they were organized primarily to provide maximum need satisfaction for the individuals who use them, with minimal waste, would not be profit-producing—are skewed in our culture in the grotesque ways that they are: toward the huge and often overbuilt hospital plants, toward gigantic and costly airplanes with high fuel consumption, toward an appallingly wasteful private-automobile industry, which becomes increasingly entrenched as alternative forms of transport are cut off. These are some of the commodity fetishisms, the sacrificing of human needs and values to the needs of the dominant economic system, that we can understand better once we grasp the broadly Marxian approach to social explanation that I have been outlining.

133

The second sort of cultural phenomenon that this approach enables us to understand is not, after all, radically discontinuous with the first, but it is sufficiently different, special, and important, particularly for theorists, to warrant separate consideration. It is the domain of ideology and of theory in general. There are some extremely interesting areas of controversy surrounding the use of the word *ideology* in Marxist and neo-Marxist thought. For example, is all present-day theory necessarily ideological, or is there, as Althusser holds [2,3], ideology on the one hand and science, exemplified by many of his own claims, on the other? By speaking of "ideology and of theory in general" I hope to circumvent those controversies. (In fact, I regard Althusser's position on this point to be more nearly correct than the opposing position as I have defined it, but not for many of the reasons that he gives.) Certainly, it is important to note that *ideology* had a pejorative connotation for Marx, and I use the word here in a somewhat pejorative way. What it connotes, at the least, is the pretense of many theorists in philosophy and various areas of the social and natural sciences to be developing purely objective accounts in complete abstraction from private interests, social and political pressures, and the general state of their existing culture. And the value of the Marxian approach to culture that I have been outlining is precisely the fact that it constantly questions this pretense.

Even the best minds have an almost inexhaustible capacity for self-deception. The most blatantly ideological forms of writing, of course, are often self-conscious and deliberate, but there is much theorizing that can be shown to be ideological, in the sense that I have just defined, without the theorist's being aware of it. And this may hold for a great philosopher such as Kant as well as for a "vulgar" (in Marx's sense) economist such as, let us say, Paul Samuelson. Kantian epistemology, like Lockean social theory, is intimately related to its entire socioeconomic setting and cannot be fully grasped without referring to that setting. Two prominent twentieth-century writers, György Lukács and C. B. Macpherson, have attempted to show this with reference to Kant [70] and Locke [91], respectively. Macpherson is not a Marxist at all in terms of his overall political theory, and Lukács, certainly at the time that he wrote *History and Class-Consciousness,* was almost as much influenced by Hegel as he was by Marx. (In fact, some of Hegel's observations about Enlightenment culture in his *Phenomenology* are very much in keeping with the approach to explanation, which I have called "broadly Marxian," that I have been discussing, except that Hegel's awareness of the more strictly economic factors is greatly underdeveloped.) I am not claiming that either Lukács's discussion of Kant or Macpherson's analysis of Locke is at all perfect—Lukács, in particular, seems to me somewhat confused in his presentation—but only that they serve as *illustrations* of the sort of analysis that can be undertaken on the basis of the insights about the relationship of socioeconomic factors to other broadly cultural phenomena that I have been discussing. This can all be done without becoming involved in the foolish and ultimately meaningless model of base and superstructure, rigidly divided and assigned different functions, that Marx and Engels unfortunately entertained in *The German Ideology* and that Soviet Marxism even more unfortunately came to fetishize. Once we abandon that model and recognize the inevitable reciprocity of the interaction between base and superstructure, we save much needless diversion of philosophical effort away from what really needs to be said by way of cultural critique.

I believe not only that the approach I have been outlining *can* be employed in understanding philosophy and theory in general, but that it *should* be. To refer to an example that I mentioned earlier, it might be an interesting exercise to treat a text of Descartes's, for instance, as if it had fallen out of the sky and had nothing to do with the society in which Descartes lived. But if this exercise is thought to furnish us with the real, "essential" Descartes, then it is radically distortive and abstract. Far from damaging philosophy's integrity, then, as the critics would claim, the approach to philosophical explanation through socioeconomic phenomena is the only fully comprehensive approach. It can be undertaken, I maintain, without reducing complex concepts to the status of counters in a warlike game after the fashion of some Marxist-Leninist polemicists.

The dominance of the economic is real enough in our lives. Cutbacks of all sorts are widespread—in services, in schools, in the arts, and so on. Inflation is unchecked and large-scale unemployment threatens. There are, to be sure, ups and downs in our economy and the economies of Western Europe on a month-by-month basis, but on the whole the situation is grim, with no prospect of sudden improvement. Even if there were a sudden if temporary improvement (such as the one that took place briefly in England in the mid-seventies on the basis of the discovery of oil), the long-range prospect continues to be of having our lives governed by the demands of the system in its very ups and downs.

Meanwhile, however, there is a strong tendency to kill, or at least severely maim, the messengers who bear the bad news. It seems plausible, superficially speaking, that persons adopting the broadly Marxist approach that I have been outlining would be especially listened to at a time when the dominance of the economic to which they have been pointing has become so obvious that no one can possibly miss it. But something rather the *opposite* of this has been occurring. I have already mentioned the situation in Germany. It may be worth mentioning a couple of interesting recent developments in two other countries, Great Britain and France, before returning to the United States.

In Great Britain, a document entitled *The Attack on Higher Education* has been the subject of considerable discussion. It is a "report" prepared in 1977 by a group of university professors and administrators, including some well-known names, that contends that Marxism, and particularly Marxist sociology, has been destructive of intellectual standards in that country. I have read this document, and I must say that I have seldom seen anything written by persons with academic training in recent years that falls so squarely within the Marxian category of "ideology." But it has been publicized by the press, and it has had its effect.

In France, a great deal has been made in recent years of the wave of so-called New Philosophers. One of the leading pieces of literature by this group is a book entitled *Les Maîtres penseurs* [45], published in 1977 by André Glucksmann. In an earlier period Glucksmann had already made a name for himself as a radical Maoist polemicist, and he is still a relatively young man. To read *Les Maîtres penseurs* as it surveys the leading figures of nineteenth-century Continental thought—Hegel, Marx, Nietzsche—is to observe the disintegration of the standards of scholarly objectivity that most of us try to maintain and hand down to our students as a very part of, rather than in opposition to, the strong positions we may hold. Barbarism—

to parody the title of a book, *La Barbarie à visage humain*, by a colleague of Glucksmann's [68]—may be elegantly dressed and even featured, as Glucksmann's was, for reasons that were anything but subtle in light of the then forthcoming national elections, on the French state television network. There is no clear dividing line "in nature" between true social and political theory and mere Tractarianism and sloganizing; any classification in this regard must be made on the basis of relative quality of thought and seriousness. The writings of the New Philosophers, like those of the eighteenth-century philosophes, lie in this border area. Unlike their distinguished predecessors, however, the New Philosophers have nothing to say, and their fad will soon pass—if indeed this process has not already begun. But the very existence of this fad is one more significant manifestation of the temper of our times.

Another illustration of similar tendencies is a *Time* magazine article published in the summer of 1977, run as the cover story in the European editions but not in the domestic edition, on "the death of Marx" [166]. The article features the New Philosophers among others. One's level of political naiveté would have to be extremely high in order to miss the propagandistic aspects of the article—the sense in which it is advocacy of a hoped-for murder, rather than reportage of a demise that has already occurred. Certainly *interest* in Marx and his thought is in many countries higher than ever before, if the familiar scientific techniques of content analysis of publications such as that issue of *Time* and similar criteria are used as guides. Nevertheless, I find myself wondering whether there may not be some truth to *Time*'s allegation after all, in light of current trends. I agree, as I hope my earlier chapters have indicated, with the broad statement that Sartre made at the outset of *Search for a Method* to the effect that Marxism is the dominant philosophy of our epoch. I believe this is still true, some twenty years after the publication of that book, even though Sartre himself may now harbor doubts about its truth. But there are at least two senses of *is* that might be distinguished in the claim "Marxism is the dominant philosophy": one, that some version of Marxism best explains many of the occurrences in the social world around us; and two, that Marxism simply is what concerns a great many people, perhaps more than any comparable world view. I have no doubts about the continued applicability of the claim in the first sense, but I sometimes wonder about the applicability of the second, perhaps not right now, but maybe a few years hence.

At any rate, the bits of evidence of a turn to the Right in the contemporary United States are unmistakable, although what they signify for the future remains very much of an enigma. The backlash against the Equal Rights Amendment and other rights claims, the widespread opposition to funding public education, and the series of Supreme Court decisions that generally seem to uphold the claims of private property against the assertions of consumer groups and other felt needs all point in a similar, reactionary direction. So do the successes of such seemingly disparate but in fact quite similar writers as Robert Nozick and Marabel Morgan. But more salient, perhaps, than these straws in the wind or the occasional showing of legitimate public revolt that ends up serving the cause of reaction more than that of radical change (the California "taxpayers' revolt," for example) is the contemporary pervasive apathy. It is not primarily an apathy of smugness, as much of the apathy in the 1950s was, but more an apathy of serial impotence.

Certainly the situation that Sartre describes in the later pages of his *Critique of Dialectical Reason,* wherein groups degenerate, is very widespread. The majority of the most active groups today are groups of the Right, not of the Left or Center—a possibility for which Sartre, of course, is perfectly capable of allowing within the framework of his theory. In our land, as in others, there is a loss of direction, a sense of drift. But this may well be temporary.

To bring this situation down to as concrete a level as possible, I shall analyze a particular subject with which I am especially familiar—the state of academic jobs in philosophy today. I take this as an *example,* an *illustration,* of the kinds of problems that are widespread in our culture. But it is of special interest, not only because I, like some of my readers, am an academic philosopher, but also because philosophy has always had a special role, a *critical* role, in Western society. One way of describing what is happening is to say that the meaning and purpose of human labor are undergoing fundamental reconsideration, more often than not without the laborers' being fully aware of or even desiring it. What makes philosophy an interesting special case within this context is that it is one of the very few activities (and in some sense the only one) in which engaging in such reconsideration has often been regarded as part of the job description.

The current state of affairs in philosophy is in many respects appalling. Good, qualified people are failing to find jobs, cutbacks are widespread, and so on: anyone familiar with the situation can fill in the details. How did this state of affairs come about? The general outlines of its etiology are well known, though there may be disagreement as to the factors to which greatest weight should be attached.

During the late 1950s and the 1960s there was a marked upsurge of interest in higher education in the United States. The generally unanticipated Soviet successes in space technology stimulated demands in this country that students be offered incentives to pursue careers in the sciences. Both the federal government and private foundations responded to these demands with such arrangements as the National Defense Education Act scholarships. The benefits of these schemes were frequently extended to aspiring young humanists, including philosophers, as well as to science students. New graduate programs were created in many institutions to cope with the rapidly expanding supply of Ph.D. candidates. Concomitantly, new undergraduate institutions, both four- and two-year, were created in large numbers. These were heady years, when the increased demands for staff members on the part of older and newer institutions alike could barely be met by the graduate schools. In a sellers' market, the buyers often made concessions: higher pay, larger fringe benefits, more frequent leaves of absence, fewer required teaching hours; the leaves and reduced teaching, in turn, increased staff sizes still further.

So much for the genesis of the "boom"; now let us summarize the "bust." It seems, in retrospect, that a presumption of systematic unlimited expansion had dominated much planning in the field of education during the period in question. While unlimited expansion may indeed be the underlying tendency of the capitalist economic system as a whole, the absurd expectation that the system will in fact continue operating uninterruptedly in accordance with this tendency for an indefinitely long time neglects a vast number of internal countervailing tendencies. We are now reaping the fruits of that neglect. Insufficient attention had been paid to population trends; only slowly did the awareness arise that the rate of growth in the number of college-age persons would undergo a drastic reduction. Meanwhile, the expansion and then gradual termination of American military operations in Indochina produced several interrelated results: a vast conscription, followed by the influx of most ex-conscripts into the job market; protests by students and professors, followed by anger against the universities on the part of members of the population who held the power of the purse; a huge investment in the armaments industry, followed by dislocations in several segments of that industry at war's end; and finally, a national mood of disenchantment with previously held values, often expressed as a reactionary opposition to programs of social welfare and as a renewed interest (to which I have already referred) in variants of outmoded classical liberal ideologies.

The current state of affairs in American philosophy, then, should occasion no surprise whatsoever. At present, relatively few college or university administrators are planning to hire more philosophers. In a "labor-intensive" industry such as theirs, administrators are now under pressure, with rare exceptions, to retrench with respect to existing positions, or at least not to expand. Under these circumstances, criteria of *efficiency* are applied with considerable strictness. This means that departments with low or declining faculty:student ratios are treated with special disfavor, and philosophy departments today frequently fall into this category (for reasons to which I shall return later), although there are a number of exceptions, owing to local conditions (for example, philosophy course requirements in the bachelor's-degree program). Even greater retrenchments would occur within professional philosophy as a result of pressures for efficiency if it were not for tenure rules, the threat of faculty unionization, and here and there a heroic gesture of goodwill on the part of some academic dean, provost, or president. Given our economic system and the events of very recent history, the inevitability of all these familiar phenomena appears so overwhelming that one is justified in questioning the value of *any* effort at transcending the present situation toward a different future.

This mood of self-doubt is widespread within American professional philosophy today. One has only, for instance, to compare the minutes of the Eastern or Western Division meetings of the American Philosophical Association in 1975–76 with those of 1968–69 to see that an atmosphere of fervid activity and involvement in national and international political issues has given way, within just a short time, to a spirit of almost total acquiescence and apathy. Colleagues from other institutions often tell me of their efforts to discourage undergraduates from choosing philosophy as their major field. The shrug of the shoulders has become the most characteristic professional gesture. *Fata volentem ducunt, nolentem trahunt;* being dragged, rather than led, by historical inevitability appears to be the dominant professional stance—especially, in my experience, among those who at the same time vehemently deny that there is a shred of truth to the notion of historical inevitability.

We need to reflect more on the situation; having done so, we shall see the need, I think, to act to change it. I propose the following theses aimed at the reform of attitudes toward professional philosophy and of the postures of professional philosophers in the United States today:

1. The discipline of philosophy is unique among academic disciplines in its commitment to the radical questioning of all presuppositions. It alone has no raison d'être apart from such an enterprise, no separate body of knowledge that it needs to preserve.

2. Philosophy is thus inherently opposed to the ideological stance of professionalism, the notion that certain individuals have a special *Competence*,* stemming from native talent or elitist training or both, that gives them authority over other human beings.

3. Nevertheless, as long as professionalism and related repressive ideological stances—racism, sexism, the cult of competitiveness, indeed a commitment to maintaining relationships of dominance and subordination of any kind—remain widespread, philosophers will themselves have an obligation to preserve a special disciplinary identity. Hence, talk of "pro-

---

*Robert A. Dahl, the political scientist, lists "Competence" as one of his three "Criteria for Authority" [29]. I am thinking here of his apparently commonsensical defense of this criterion, to which, it should be clear, I believe serious exception should be taken.

fessional philosophy" remains meaningful today and will continue to be so for the foreseeable future.

4. Professional philosophers, in subspecialties as diverse as ethics, metaphysics, the philosophy of law, and logic, perform a function in keeping with the historical role of philosophy only to the extent that they share a commitment to the radical questioning of presuppositions. Those employed as philosophers who regard themselves as having discharged their responsibilities when they have rung a few changes on the doctrines of Plato, Saint Thomas, Kant, Heidegger, Austin, or any other historical or contemporary figure—or on any methodology, language, or other body of knowledge (e.g., modern-day physical theory) considered canonical—are in fact derelict.

5. But there can be no comprehension of the presuppositions to be questioned in any domain of beliefs without a knowledge of the history of philosophy, including recent contemporary philosophy. Consequently, soi-disant professional philosophers who denigrate such knowledge are equally derelict.

6. Philosophy, construed along the lines just delineated, is and will remain for an indefinite time to come an essential constituent of culture, if *culture* is defined as the exploration and cognition of the most diverse possibilities of human activity in the present and future and of the most diverse achievements in the past. To the extent that colleges and universities remain important vehicles for passing on and generating culture, such institutions must strongly encourage the teaching and study of philosophy so construed.

7. But such a policy of encouraging philosophy is in contradiction with the principal raison d'être of educational institutions within the framework of a capitalist economy, that raison d'être being to facilitate *productivity*, understood in its capitalist sense (the making of goods to create maximum profits), by training managers, technologists, civil servants, and so on.

8. Professional philosophers and other sympathetic educators, having recognized the existence of this contradiction, must at once cope with it in the present and look to its future overcoming within the framework of a different economic system, whose conception of productivity will be more congenial to their endeavors.

I think it highly possible to justify almost all the subspecialties in the field of philosophy that are engaged in today by those paid to philosophize—including, certainly, even esoteric forms of logic and the analysis of ordinary language—in accordance with the conception of philosophy that I have outlined in my theses. But such justification cannot be taken for granted. A philosopher who is not self-conscious about his or her social role as a philosopher is a contradiction in terms; practically speaking, however, many such living contradictions exist—individuals in whom the level of self-consciousness concerning their professional practice is, at best, very low. The only remedy for this condition, if I am correct in my claim that it exists, is widespread consciousness raising on the theme "Why philosophy?" or "Why philosophers?," and it is the past and present tradition of social and political philosophy that is best equipped to lead this endeavor. Only those who have undertaken such self-examination and who have reached a nonskeptical conclusion can have any claim to receive a share of scarce social resources, in the form of wages for skilled labor, for their work as philosophers.

The range of possible nonskeptical conclusions is, to be sure, quite broad. Within that range, the defense of philosophy as a watchdog of the established socioeconomic order is one possible conclusion. Indeed, it is a conclusion that has been reached many times in the past, often by the most articulate social and political philosophers. Hegel's *Philosophy of Right* is the most nearly perfect, most self-conscious historical expression of such a position. But this perfect example of philosophy-as-watchdog is also, as my analysis at the beginning of chapter two indicates, the strongest argument against despairing of philosophy's social and cultural role as radical critic of the established order; for no serious student of Marx and Hegel has any difficulty in seeing Marx as Hegel's philosophical heir, through a dialectical thought process (corresponding to changing material conditions) that was clearly anticipated in many of Hegel's passages. The lesson to be drawn from this, I think, is that those who support the employment of philosophy as radical critic of social orders should not become too discouraged about the existence of philosopher-watchdogs. For the best, most consistent of watchdogs are capable of turning, or of being turned, against guardians or institutions that prove to be unworthy.

In short, professional philosophy deserves to be championed as a crucial element in the culture of the immediate future

143

only to the extent that increasing numbers of professional philosophers become increasingly self-conscious of the social relevance of their discipline. Without further elaborating here on
the infra-disciplinary aspect of the question of what is to be
done (my aim is to be provocative, not exhaustive), I shall turn,
finally, to the external aspect. It is at this point that generalized
theory and proposed practice reencounter dismal fact: the current job crisis, regarded as part of the current cultural crisis,
with which I began.

It is an elementary mistake, one that in my experience is
frequently repeated in these depressing times, to say that the
job crisis is *simply* a function of declining student demands, in
the form of decreasing enrollments in philosophy courses,
combined with an excess supply of (technically) qualified instructors. It would be perfectly possible, for example, for educational administrators to decide that the special character of
philosophy as a discipline requires a very low ratio of faculty
members to students; or for foundations and/or governmental
agencies to fund the establishment of large research institutes
in philosophy, employing dozens or even hundreds of Ph.D.
holders; or for faculties throughout the country to reinstate
philosophy course requirements for the bachelor's degree.
These are only three of many possibilities. None is really farfetched; all have precedents both in philosophy and, even
more so, in other fields. The point is that the so-called law of
supply and demand, in education as in other areas of the economy, is by itself a tautology, or very nearly so, capable of
explaining nothing (as Marx pointed out long ago in *Capital*
[102]): it obtains only after all the assumptions as to what constitutes supply, and what demand, have been stipulated. Of
course, there are outer limits of a sort. A society at our stage of
technological development that suddenly "decided," collec-
tively, to allocate the major part of the surplus-value generated
within industry to the financing of armies of professional philosophers would suffer some fairly severe dislocations for a
time. But there is nothing inconceivable or technically infeasi-
ble about such a move.

The immediate practical value of such speculation is to re-
mind us that there are many more variables, in assessing the
possible future course of the job market, than simply enroll-
ment and demographic statistics. The practical *significance* of

144

these and all such statistics is determined by social structures; and social structures are changeable, though seldom with ease. Even the projections of future college-age populations—as popular now, when they are being taken to portend decline, as they were disregarded in the palmy, expansionist 1960s—are absolute only in a relative sense; they depend, that is, on un- provable assumptions about the approximate constancy of the percentage of high-school graduates who will go on to college in the coming years. In fact, as the educational Malthusians themselves are apt to point out, that percentage may decline as the costs of education increase and the relative financial ad- vantages of higher degrees can be demonstrated, in a generally poor employment situation, to be diminishing. Colleges and universities would then have even fewer students than antici- pated in the coming decades. And where would that leave, among others, the poor professional philosopher?

It *could* leave her or him in a position to lead the way in reasserting the possibility that human lives can be orientated toward purposes other than those of profit maximization (or, minimally, of competitive survival), dictated by the capitalist economic system within which we all operate at present. Mod- ern American universities have generally shaped their policies to conform to those demands as the demands affect the process of training new generations of functionaries for this system. By an understandable but still shocking paradox, this tendency has become more focused and obvious as the system passes through a period of severe malfunctioning: we are all familiar with the cycle to which I have already referred—general job shortage, desperate desire on students' parts to produce the maximally "salable" transcript, response on the part of counsel- ors and administrators in the form of advocating (often reluc- tantly, of course) that students take greater numbers of techni- cal, preprofessional, so-called practical courses at the expense of courses in the humanities. Now, perhaps, we are moving toward a period when the claim that higher education is worth- while because it "pays off" financially will cease to be valid, or at any rate will be valid only in a marginal way, for large numbers of potential college students. As this happens, the individuals who are supposed to question presuppositions and values, the philosophers, are in principle well suited to retain their intellectual composure and to assist administrators and

145

other academics in radically reexamining the functions of the academy.

Institutions of higher education preexisted the modern capitalist world, and they retain certain residues of their earlier forms. This is a major reason, of course, for the fact that present-day colleges and universities are even now not *totally* integrated within our socioeconomic system, as evidenced by their retaining subjects of very marginal value for the system's purposes, such as philosophy. The situation thus characterized is a potentially promising one for supporting a radical *mise en question* of the assumptions of the system itself.

In order for such a move to take place over a necessarily sustained period of time, it is essential that a large core of intellectually gifted individuals, imbued with a knowledge of our culture's past (together with, one hopes, some familiarity with other cultures) and with a strong capacity to conceive of alternatives to any given state of affairs, be present within our academic institutions. It may well be, as was recently urged on me in an argument against becoming greatly concerned about the job crisis, that the existence of large numbers of unemployed and presumably discontented philosophy Ph.D.'s could create an "interesting" situation, with the potential for an increased radical consciousness. But our society is so vast that the chance that such individuals, at best numerically quite small in *relative* size, could have a significant social impact is not great. Moreover, to speak only of this social aspect of the argument is to neglect the important dimension of the happiness of the affected individuals. My own practical conclusion is that one should strive vigorously simultaneously to encourage the study of philosophy and the employment of philosophers as philosophers. The obstacles presented by tight budgets and many related factors are severe, to be sure; but such obstacles are not always as rigid as they appear, and the alternative of passive acquiescence is unacceptable if one cares about society's future.

For this is the ultimate issue. We have no assurance that the recent widely acknowledged emphasis on technical training at the expense of other types of college courses will not continue or perhaps accelerate. In the long run, this will result in a smaller number of institutions of higher education than there are now and in the near disappearance of courses in philosophy (except, perhaps, for a few "service courses," such as business ethics) and related fields. No one should enter into deep mourning at the idea of the disappearance of certain institutions with which we have been familiar, since institutions have no meaning apart from the human beings who compose and sustain them. But the question is whether the positive social functions that have been served—however poorly and with however large an admixture of irrelevance and of acquiescence in the "watchdog" role—by the presence of philosophers on college faculties can be equally well served in some other setting within society. For the foreseeable future, it seems to me, that is unlikely. Consequently, the removal of philosophy from American academic life would constitute a net social loss, while the expansion of philosophy's role *could* constitute a gain.

A broad understanding of philosophy's "positive social functions" must include some reference to the definition of *culture* proposed in my sixth thesis above, namely, "the exploration and cognition of the most diverse possibilities of human activity in the present and future and of the most diverse achievements in the past." The loss of philosophers, without the concomitant growth of some other group committed to doing more or less what the best philosophers today do, would mean nothing less than the loss (in the sense of a diminution of the level) of human culture itself within our society—a narrowing of society's collective recognition of its range of possibilities.

One is reminded of Socrates' dictum that the unexamined life is not worth living. This applies at least as much to the life of a society as it does to an individual's life. If our society moves in the direction of disvaluing the Socratic role and making it impossible to fill, by eliminating employment possibilities for those capable of filling it while continuing to make the performance of wage labor a condition of survival, then society will, in keeping with Nietzsche's worst fears, be reducing its own purpose to that of the void.

The preceding analysis of the situation of professional philosophy, considered as an aspect of contemporary culture that is, like so many aspects of that culture, in a state of crisis, should be taken to illustrate the use of the approach to social explanation that I have been advocating. As an illustration, it is

147

far from comprehensive; my adoption of a thesis style in the middle of it signifies that there has been a drastic, intentional foreshortening. However, as an illustration it may still be illuminating. Of necessity, it is somewhat narcissistic and self-indulgent: theory theorizing about itself. But it can also be regarded in a less harsh light. It may be said to exemplify a notion of theory that takes theory itself as one among several types of labor, of social activity—as a cultural phenomenon—rather than as the privileged product of an ideal and essentially atemporal world.

The analysis can obviously be extended, without much alteration, to encompass both other areas of the humanities besides philosophy and the more theoretical components of some of the social sciences, notably political science, to the extent to which these are also understood as kinds of work for which a few individuals in our society still receive salaries. Many additional variants would have to be introduced in order to extend the same sort of analysis to those other academic workers whose jobs can be defined as the study of one or another mood of Plato's "great, strong beast"—the majority of social scientists and particularly of professional economists. In the lives of such individuals, too, of course, what I have been calling "the dominance of the economic" is a prominent reality; indeed, some of them are apt to be more consciously aware of this than is the type of professional humanist who regards his or her activity as essentially privileged and otherworldly. But these nonhumanistic workers have, as a group, profited from the social structures that I have described to a degree that the humanists have not. This remains true, though less clearly so than it was, let us say, a decade and a half ago. There are now serious job shortages in a number of the social-science professions, not simply because of an overproduction of graduate degrees, but also, and equally, because of reductions in funding.

Other types of work activity that are primarily or in large measure university-based, such as research in some of the natural sciences, could likewise be analyzed in a similar fashion, but with additional variations to take account of both their intrinsic peculiarities and, particularly, their relationships to the demands and mechanisms of our socioeconomic system. But university-based activity, while it is unquestionably of disproportionate importance for understanding our society's nature and the directions that its development is taking, accounts for only a small portion of its total work activity. Political economy, from Smith through Marx and beyond, tended to focus on *industrial production* as the paradigmatic work activity of the modern world. It still is, but less clearly so than in the recent past. Any fruitful new theoretical analysis of the role of industrial production in contemporary culture must concern itself with factors that were of relatively less importance in the past, and with one above all: oil. A number of other types of work, however, offer more abundant possibilities for theoretically informed analysis of a comparatively novel sort; transportation, health care, and elementary and secondary education are three good examples. Individuals involved in all three generally share something of the sense of crisis that is prevalent in academic philosophy and in most of the rest of higher education today and that is not so widespread, at least at the time of this writing (winter 1979), in industry. All of these fields are of great importance in determining the character of our culture, in the broad sense that I have been using that word.

The approach that I am advocating does not attempt to shun advocacy. My theses directed toward the reform of attitudes and postures in contemporary professional philosophy exemplify this. However, the starting point and principal focus must remain descriptive and analytic rather than exhortatory, with any resulting "exhortation" being based, essentially, in a description of future possibilities. (This, too, is in accord with the Continental philosophical tradition of Marx, Sartre, and others, as I have shown with respect to Marx in my treatment [83] of his "Vision of a Possible Future.") If, as I assume, the human future is not inexorably predetermined in a single direction, then our culture may evolve in a number of different ways. It should be the business of the theorist both to indicate some of the more salient future possibilities and, if my broad view of *theory* as including a normative element is accepted, to render her or his evaluations of these alternatives.

At present, it is unwise to be too sanguine about the resolutions of its crisis upon which our culture will settle. I have consistently used the expression *our culture* in the loose sense that I defined in the first paragraph of this chapter: the culture that is, for what I consider factual reasons, primarily American- (i.e., United States-) oriented and secondarily West European-oriented. Of course, political decisions by governments, and not necessarily only those in the culturally dominant regions, can have severe short-term effects on this culture, especially when such decisions concern military actions in an age of super-weapons. In the limiting case, that of global hydrogen holocaust, one possible set of decisions would effect the termination of all human life and hence, a fortiori, of culture itself. There are other ways (chemical catastrophe, uncontrollable fatal disease, collision of planets) in which it is conceivable that the same outcome could be achieved, as it no doubt eventually will be, in one way or another, whether in a year or many eons hence. However, absent such extreme possibilities, one cannot regard episodic political decisions or the momentary electoral victory of one party as playing the most decisive roles in determining the long-term course of historical development. It is in the deeper contemporary cultural trends, some of which I have documented in this chapter, rather than in the passing fashions of the current, generally undistinguished generation of political leaders, that I believe the stronger grounds for pessimism lie.

People who are convinced that they are in a desperate struggle to retain the level of need satisfaction that they have achieved are poor prospects for cultivating theoretical discussions of the long-term future. Far from worrying about, for example, the conceptual inadequacies of the classical notion of the "common good" when applied to a class-divided society, they are apt to wish to purge entirely from their consideration all social issues that do not appear to affect them directly and immediately. This is the condition of our society today. Meanwhile, we have our complement of ideologists who assure us that only individual interests are real, anyway, so why worry? These ideologists often enough even call themselves social theorists. In such a climate it is not easy to uphold the value of a critical approach to society of the sort that I have been defending in this book; even the very modest version of it that I have discerned as emanating from new trends in the philosophy of law is likely to encounter considerable hostility and/or indifference.

But the generalizations that I have just written concerning likely aggregate behavior of individuals in a society characterized by the socioeconomic conditions that characterize ours today are at best bits of "pop psychology" that in effect attempt to elevate a description of the current cultural climate into a set of allegedly universal laws. They are themselves little better than scattered propositions about the surface moods and wants of the "great, strong beast" of the very sort to which Plato was referring. However, it has been the common assumption, whether implicit or explicit, of social theorists from Plato on that social theory consists of something more than just this. And it is a necessarily correlative assumption, for all except those theorist who are content to construct purely utopian schemes, that the perceived moods and wants of the social animal at a given place and time are not permanently fixed within any certain range, but rather are capable of undergoing fundamental change. That assumption alone allows for a modicum of optimism.

Conclusion

This book has been written assertively and in places no doubt even dogmatically. Nevertheless, it has been composed with a view to opening a dialogue with my readers. For I obviously regard many of the issues upon which I have touched as of crucial importance for our world.

The purpose of the first chapter was to present information—to convey *my* comprehension, at least, of the principal trends in social and political theory in the major Western countries over the last thirty years, primarily since the end of World War II. What I tried to show was, first, the continued though uneasy acceptance, in social theory within the social sciences, of the idea satirized long ago by Plato that what was most needed was an uncritical study of the moods and wants of the "great, strong beast" that is the state or society; second, the somewhat encouraging revival of social and political philosophy in England and, by derivation, the United States after a period known as "the heyday of Weldonism," during which political philosophy was asserted to be dead; and third, the dominant force of Marxism in Continental European social and political philosophy throughout this period. I stated, and tried at several points to show, that none of these theoretical developments occurred in abstraction from other social and historical events of their times, and that there were in fact close correlations between the theoretical developments and the other events. However, I could only assert this, not having brought in any of the intellectual apparatus that would provide *understanding* of why this might be the case.

The second chapter treated the one recent work in the whole field of social and political theory—Sartre's *Critique of Dialectical Reason*—that seems to provide the most serviceable such intellectual apparatus. I pointed out some of the ways in which,

153

despite its originality and currentness, it also falls within a long tradition of social and political philosophy that includes the great figures of both Hegel and Marx. The book's strengths and shortcomings were discussed.

The third chapter covered the briefer tradition of the philosophy of law by way of introducing the work that has dominated contemporary social- and political-philosophy discussions in the United States and England, John Rawls's *A Theory of Justice*. I showed that Rawls's approach, at once excessively general or formal and excessively specific or provincial—which is consonant with much of traditional legal philosophy—is deficient because of its failure to base itself on concrete injustices and wrongs. I suggested that some new trends in the philosophy of law, including ideas found in Ronald Dworkin's collection of essays, *Taking Rights Seriously*, are more encouraging. But I also noted that Sartre, Marx, and mainstream Continental European philosophy in general since Hegel have *neglected* legal and related institutions, to their own detriment, just as the principal Anglo-American works have grossly ignored the entire Continental tradition. A synthesis thus seems to be called for.

The fourth and final chapter moved furthest in the direction of concrete current events. I tried to show—through a reference to Marcuse's classic of the 1960s, *One-Dimensional Man*, through a discussion of a broadly Marxian and Sartrean approach to explanation in terms of socioeconomic factors, and then through a detailed examination of the academic-job crisis in philosophy—how social and political philosophy can be employed both to understand where we as a society really are and how we might go about improving on our present, rather grim position. But I also brought out evidence that our society may be in the process of rejecting the intellectual tools that are needed to do these things—such tools being the intellectual traditions, best represented by Marx and Sartre, that I have highlighted in this book.

Thus we are at a crossroads, in theory and in practice. If social and political philosophy is entering a period of quiescence, as there are some disturbing signs that it may be, this event might be seen as an important symptom of, and a contributing factor to, a period of further cultural regressions and crisis. If social and political philosophy continues to experience

Conclusion

a resurgence, then that will be a good indication that our culture itself is embarking on a path of revitalization. No one today is endowed with a gift of prophecy adequate to disclose which of these alternatives will come about.

Notes

(1) ALLEN, DEREK P. H.
"Distributive Justice and Utilitarian Justification in Classical Marxism."
Unpublished ms. University of Toronto, 1978.

ALTHUSSER, LOUIS
(2) *For Marx,* tr. Ben Brewster.
New York. Random House, 1970.
(3) *Lenin and Philosophy and Other Essays,* tr. Ben Brewster.
New York. Monthly Review Press, 1971.
(4) *American Political Science Review* 69, 2 (June 1975): 588–674.
(5) ANDERSON, PERRY.
"Components of the National Culture."
In Cockburn, Alexander, and Blackburn, Robin, eds.
Student Power.
Harmondsworth. Penguin Books, 1969: 214–284.

ARENDT, HANNAH.
(6) *Between Past and Future: Eight Exercises in Political Thought.*
New York. Viking Press, 1968.
(7) *The Human Condition.*
Chicago. University of Chicago Press, 1958.
(8) *The Origins of Totalitarianism,* second enlarged edition.
Cleveland. World Publishing Co., 1958.
(9) ARON, RAYMOND.
The Opium of the Intellectuals, tr. Terence Kilmartin.
New York. W. W. Norton, 1962.
(10) ARROW, KENNETH.
"Some Ordinalist-Utilitarian Notes on Rawls's Theory of Justice."
Journal of Philosophy 70, 9 (May 10, 1973): 245–263.
(11) AVINERI, SHLOMO.
Hegel's Theory of the Modern State.
Cambridge. At the University Press, 1973.

157

Notes

(12) AXELOS, KOSTAS.
Alienation, Praxis, and Technē in the Thought of Karl Marx, tr. Ronald Bruzina.
Austin. University of Texas Press, 1976.

(13) AYER, A. J.
Language, Truth, and Logic.
London. Gollancz, 1936.

(14) BABB, H. W., ed. and tr.
Soviet Legal Philosophy.
Cambridge. Harvard University Press, 1951.

(15) BARRY, BRIAN.
The Liberal Theory of Justice.
Oxford. At the Clarendon Press, 1973.

(16) BAY, CHRISTIAN.
The Structure of Freedom.
Palo Alto. Stanford University Press, 1958.

(17) BECKWITH, D.
"Treating People As Equals."
Time 110 (September 5, 1977): 54.

(18) BENTLEY, ARTHUR F.
The Process of Government: Political Interests and Public Opinion.
Chicago. University of Chicago Press, 1908.

(19) BERLIN, ISAIAH.
"Does Political Theory Still Exist?"
In Laslett, Peter, and Runciman, W. G., eds.
Philosophy, Politics, and Society, second series.
Oxford. Basil Blackwell, 1964: 1–33.

BERNSTEIN, RICHARD J.
The Restructuring of Social and Political Theory.
New York. Harcourt Brace Jovanovich, 1976.
(20) Pages 1–54.
(21) Pages 63–74.

(22) BOBBIO, NORBERTO.
Il positivismo giuridico.
Turin. N. Morra, undated course notes.

(23) BURNHAM, JAMES.
The Machiavellians: Defenders of Freedom.
New York. John Day Co., 1943.

CAMUS, ALBERT.
(24) Lettre au directeur des *Temps modernes.*
Les Temps modernes 82 (August 1952): 317–333.

Notes

(25) *The Rebel*, tr. Anthony Bower.
New York. Alfred A. Knopf, 1956.

(26) CHIODI, PIETRO.
Sartre and Marxism, tr. Kate Soper.
Atlantic Highlands. Humanities Press, 1976.

(27) COHN-BENDIT, DANIEL; DUTEUIL, JEAN-PIERRE; GERARD, BER-
    TRAND; and GRANAUTIER, BERTRAND.
"Why Sociologists?"
In Cockburn, Alexander, and Blackburn, Robin, eds.
Student Power.
Harmondsworth. Penguin Books, 1969: 373–378.

DAHL, ROBERT A.
(28) *After the Revolution? Authority in a Good Society*.
New Haven. Yale University Press, 1970.
(29) Pages 28–40.
(30) *A Preface to Democratic Theory*.
Chicago. University of Chicago Press, 1956.

(31) DANIELS, NORMAN, ed.
Reading Rawls.
New York. Basic Books, 1975.

DE BEAUVOIR, SIMONE.
(32) *The Ethics of Ambiguity*, tr. Bernard Frechtman.
New York. Philosophical Library, 1948.
(33) *Force of Circumstance*, tr. Richard Howard.
New York. G. P. Putnam's Sons, 1964: 385.
(34) *Memoirs of a Dutiful Daughter*, tr. James Kirkup.
Cleveland. World Publishing Co., 1959: 335.
(35) *The Second Sex*, tr. H. M. Parshley.
New York. Alfred A. Knopf, 1952.

(36) D' ENTREVES, A. P.
Natural Law: An Introduction to Legal Philosophy.
London. Hutchinson University Library, 1951: 114–116.

(37) DESAN, WILFRID.
The Marxism of Jean-Paul Sartre.
Garden City. Doubleday & Co., 1965.

(38) DWORKIN, RONALD.
Taking Rights Seriously.
Cambridge. Harvard University Press, 1977.
(39) Pages 150–183.
(40) Pages 206–222.

Notes

(41) ENGELS, FRIEDRICH.
"On the Housing Question."
In Marx, Karl, and Engels, Friedrich, *Selected Works*, vol.
Moscow. Foreign Languages Publishing House, 1962: 624.

(42) FOUCAULT, MICHEL.
Discipline and Punish: The Birth of the Prison, tr. Alan Sheri(
New York. Pantheon, 1978.

(43) FRIED, MARLENE.
"Marxism and Justice."
Unpublished ms. Bentley College, 1978.

(44) FRIEDRICH, CARL JOACHIM, ed.
Totalitarianism.
Cambridge. Harvard University Press, 1954.

(45) GLUCKSMANN, ANDRE JEAN-PIERRE.
Les Maîtres penseurs.
Paris. Grasset, 1977.

(46) GRAMSCI, ANTONIO.
Selections from the Prison Notebooks, tr. Quintin Hoare and Ge(
frey Nowell Smith.
International Publishers, 1971: 123–205.

(47) HABERMAS, JURGEN.
Knowledge and Human Interests, tr. Jeremy E. Shapiro.
Boston. Beacon Press, 1971.

(48) HAMPSHIRE, STUART.
"A New Philosophy of the Just Society."
The New York Review of Books (February 24, 1972): 34–39.

(49) HART, H. L. A.
The Concept of Law.
Oxford. At the Clarendon Press, 1961: 138–144.

HEGEL, GEORG W. F.
(50) *Natural Law*, tr. T. M. Knox.
Philadelphia. University of Pennsylvania Pres, 1975.
(51) *The Phenomenology of Mind*, tr. J. B. Baillie.
London. George Allen & Unwin, 1949: 419–438.
Philosophy of Right, tr. T. M. Knox.
Oxford. At the Clarendon Press, 1942.
(52) Page 3.
(53) Pages 148–152.
(54) Pages 16–20.
(55) Page 12.

(56) HOBBES, THOMAS.
Leviathan; Or the Matter, Forme and Power of a Commonwealth Eccle siasticall and Civil, ed. Michael Oakeshott.
Oxford. Basil Blackwell, 1950: ch. 11, 63.

(57) JAY, MARTIN.
The Dialectical Imagination.
Boston. Little, Brown and Co., 1973.

(58) KAFKA, FRANZ.
The Trial, tr. Willa Muir and Edwin Muir.
New York. Alfred A. Knopf, 1956: 267–268.

(59) KANT, IMMANUEL.
The Metaphysical Elements of Justice (Part 1 of *The Metaphysics ι Morals*), tr. John Ladd.
Indianapolis. Bobbs-Merrill Co., 1965.

KELSEN, HANS.
(60) *General Theory of Law and State*, tr. Anders Wedberg.
New York. Russell & Russell, 1961.
(61) *The Pure Theory of Law*, tr. Max Knight.
Berkeley. University of California Press, 1970.

(62) KIPNIS, KENNETH, ed.
Philosophical Issues in Law: Cases and Materials.
Englewood Cliffs. Prentice-Hall, 1977.

(63) KOSIK, KAREL.
Dialectics of the Concrete: A Study on Problems of Man and World, tr. Karel Kovanda with James Schmidt.
Dordrecht. D. Reidel Publishing Co., 1976.

(64) KUHN, THOMAS.
The Structure of Scientific Revolutions.
Chicago. University of Chicago Press, 1962.

(65) LANE, ROBERT.
Political Ideology: Why the American Common Man Believes What He Does.
New York. Free Press of Glencoe, 1962.

(66) LASSWELL, HAROLD.
Politics: Who Gets What, When, How.
New York. McGraw-Hill Book Co., 1936.

(67) LENIN, V. I.
Materialism and Empirio-Criticism: Critical Comments on a Reactionary Philosophy.
New York. International Publishers, 1927.

161

Notes

(68) LEVY, BERNARD-HENRI.
La Barbarie à visage humain.
Paris. Grasset, 1977.

LUKÁCS, GYORGY.
History and Class-Consciousness: Studies in Marxist Dialectics, tr.
Rodney Livingstone.
M.I.T. Press, 1971.
(69) Pages 256–271.
(70) Pages 110–134.

MCBRIDE, WILLIAM LEON.
(71) "The Acceptance of a Legal System."
The Monist 49 (1965): 377–396.
(72) "The Concept of Justice in Marx, Engels, and Others."
Ethics 85, 3 (April 1975): 204–218.
(73) "The Essential Role of Models and Analogies in the Philosophy
of Law."
New York University Law Review 43, 1 (March 1968): 62–72.
*Fundamental Change in Law and Society: Hart and Sartre on Revolu-
tion.*
The Hague. Mouton, 1970.
(74) Pages 176–186.
(75) Pages 199–205.
(76) "Intellectual Productivity in Capitalist and Post-Capitalist Societies."
Praxis 1974 (1–2): 227–236.
(77) "Jean-Paul Sartre: Man, Freedom, and *Praxis.*"
In George A. Schrader, Jr., ed.
Existential Philosophers: Kierkegaard to Merleau-Ponty.
New York. McGraw-Hill, 1967: 294–307.
(78) "Marxism and Natural Law."
The American Journal of Jurisprudence 15 (1970): 129–131.
(79) "Marxism and Phenomenology."
Journal of the British Society for Phenomenology 6, 1 (January 1975):
13–22.
(80) "The Nature of Political Philosophy and the Attempt to Go Be-
yond Politics."
Akten des XIV. Internationalen Kongresses für Philosophie, vol. 5.
Vienna. Verlag Herder, 1970: 247–254.
(81) "Non-Coercive Society: Some Doubts, Leninist and Contempo-
rary."
In Pennock, J. Roland, and Chapman, John W., eds.
Coercion (Nomos 14).
Chicago/New York. Aldine-Atherton, 1972: 178–197.

Notes

The Philosophy of Marx.
London. Hutchinson & Co., 1977.
(82) Pages 116–126.
(83) Pages 127–140.
(84) "Political Theory *Sub Specie Aeternitatis:* A New Perspective."
Yale Law Journal 81, 5 (April 1972): 980–1003.
(85) Review of three books by Nicos Poulantzas.
Society 14, 4 (May–June 1977): 84–88.
(86) "Sartre and the Phenomenology of Social Violence."
In Edie, James M., ed.
New Essays in Phenomenology.
New York. Quadrangle Books, 1969: 290–313.
(87) Summer School in Korčula."
Radical Philosophers' Newsjournal 2 (March 1974): 23–34.

(88) MACDONALD, MARGARET.
"The Language of Political Theory."
In Flew, Antony, ed.
Essays on Logic and Language, first series.
Oxford. Blackwell, 1951: 176.

(89) MACHIAVELLI, NICCOLO.
The Prince, tr. Robert M. Adams.
New York. W. W. Norton, 1977: ch. 15, 44.

(90) MACPHERSON, CRAWFORD BROUGH.
The Political Theory of Possessive Individualism.
Oxford. At the Clarendon Press, 1962.
(91) Pages 194–262.

(92) MANSER, ANTHONY.
Sartre: A Philosophic Study.
London: Athlone Press, 1966.

MARCUSE, HERBERT.
(93) *Eros and Civilization: A Philosophical Inquiry into Freud.*
Boston. Beacon Press, 1955.
(94) *One-Dimensional Man: Studies in the Ideology of Advanced Industrial Society.*
Boston. Beacon Press, 1964.
(94a) Pages 256–257.
(95) *Reason and Revolution: Hegel and the Rise of Social Theory.*
Boston. Beacon Press, 1960.
(96) *Soviet Marxism: A Critical Analysis.*
New York. Random House, 1961.

MARX, KARL.
Capital: A Critical Analysis of Capitalist Production, vol. 1, tr. Samuel Moore and Edward Aveling.

Moscow. Foreign Languages Publishing House, 1961.
(97) Ch. 7, sect. 2, 194.
(98) Ch. 1, sect. 4, 77–81.
(99) Ch. 15, sect. 9, 489–490.
(100) Ch. 15, sect. 9, 487–488.
(101) Ch. 9, sect. 3, 224–229.
(102) *Capital: A Critique of Political Economy*, vol. 3, ed. Friedrich Engels.

Moscow. Foreign Languages Publishing House, 1962: ch. 10, 185–186.
(103) *Theories of Surplus Value, part 1.*

Moscow. Progress Publishers, 1961: ch. 4, sect. 3 and 4, 155–174.

MERLEAU-PONTY, MAURICE.
(104) *Adventures of the Dialectic,* tr. Joseph Bien.
Evanston. Northwestern University Press, 1973.
(105) Pages 95–201.
(106) *Humanism and Terror: An Essay on the Communist Problem,* tr. John O'Neill.
Boston. Beacon Press, 1969.
(107) *Phenomenology of Perception,* tr. Colin Smith.
London. Routledge & Kegan Paul, 1962: 442–450.

(108) NIELSEN, KAI.
"Class and Justice."
In Arthur, John, and Shaw, William, eds.
Justice and Economic Distribution.
Englewood Cliffs. Prentice-Hall, 1973: 225–245.

NOZICK, ROBERT.
(109) *Anarchy, State, and Utopia.*
New York. Basic Books, 1974.
(110) Page 352.
(111) Page xii.
(112) Distributive Justice.
Philosophy & Public Affairs 3, 1 (fall 1973): 45–126.

(113) PERELMAN, CHAIM.
Justice.
New York. Random House, 1967.

(114) PETROVIC, GAJO.
Marx in the Mid-Twentieth Century.
Garden City. Anchor Books, 1967: 171–189.

PITKIN, HANNAH.
(115) *The Concept of Representation.*

Notes

Berkeley. University of California Press, 1967.
(116) *Wittgenstein and Justice.*
    Berkeley. University of California Press, 1972.

(117) PLATO.
    Republic, tr. Allan Bloom.
    New York. Basic Books, 1968: book 6, 493a, pages 172–173.

POPPER, KARL R.
(118) *The Open Society and Its Enemies,* revised edition.
    Princeton. Princeton University Press, 1950.
(119) *The Poverty of Historicism.*
    London. Routledge & Kegan Paul, 1957.

POULANTZAS, NICOS.
(120) *Classes in Contemporary Capitalism,* tr. David Fernbach.
    Atlantic Highlands. Humanities Press, 1975.
(121) *Fascism and Dictatorship: The Third International and the Problem of Fascism,* tr. Judith White.
    Atlantic Highlands. Humanities Press, 1974.
(122) *Political Power and Social Classes,* tr. Timothy O'Hagan et al.
    Atlantic Highlands. Humanities Press, 1973.

RAWLS, JOHN.
(123) "Justice As Fairness."
    Philosophical Review 67 (1958): 164–194.
(124) *A Theory of Justice.*
    Cambridge. Harvard University Press, 1971.
(125) Page 587.
(126) Page 137.
(127) Pages 137–138.
(128) Page 302.
(129) Page 92.
(130) Page 74.
(131) Pages 152–153.
(132) Page 204.
(133) REVEL, JEAN-FRANÇOIS.
    Without Marx or Jesus: The New American Revolution Has Begun, tr. J. F. Bernard.
    Garden City. Doubleday, 1971.

(134) ROSS, ALF.
    On Law and Justice.
    Berkeley. University of California Press, 1959.

(135) RUNCIMAN, W. G.
    "Sociological Evidence and Political Theory."
    In Laslett, Peter, and Runciman, W. G.

Notes

Philosophy, Politics, and Society, Second series.
Oxford. Basil Blackwell, 1964: 34.

SARTRE, JEAN-PAUL.

(136) Anti-Semite and Jew, tr. George J. Becker.
New York. Schocken Books, 1965.

(137) *Being and Nothingness: An Essay on Phenomenological Ontology,* tr.
Hazel E. Barnes.
New York. Philosophical Library, 1956: 221–430.

(138) "Childhood of a Leader."
In *Intimacy, and Other Stories,* tr. Lloyd Alexander.
New York. New Directions, 1948.

(139) *The Communists and Peace. With a Reply to Claude Lefort,* tr. Martha
H. Fletcher with John R. Kleinschmidt.
New York. G. Braziller, 1968.
Critique of Dialectical Reason, vol. 1, *Theory of Practical Ensembles,*
tr. Alan Sheridan-Smith.
London. NLB, 1976.

(140) Page 125.

(141) Pages 247–250.

(142) Pages 485–486.

(143) Page 307.

(144) Page 227.

(145) Page 357.

(146) Page 309.

(147) *Existentialism,* tr. Bernard Frechtman.
New York. Philosophical Library, 1947.

(148) *The Ghost of Stalin,* tr. Martha H. Fletcher with John R. Kleinschmidt.
New York. G. Braziller, 1968.

(149) *L'Idiot de la famille: Gustave Flaubert de 1821 à 1857,* 3 vols.
Paris. Editions Gallimard, 1971–1972.

(150) "Materialism and Revolution."
In *Literary and Philosophical Essays,* tr. Annette Michelson.
New York. Criterion Books, 1955: 198–256.

(151) *Nausea,* tr. Lloyd Alexander.
New York. New Directions, 1964: 82–94.
Search for a Method, tr. Hazel E. Barnes.
New York. Alfred A. Knopf, 1963.

(152) Page 7.

(153) Page 62.

(154) Page 31.

(155) "Socialism in One Country."
New Left Review 100 (November 1976): 143–163.

Notes

(156) *The Transcendence of the Ego: An Existentialist Theory of Conscious-*
     ness, tr. Forrest Williams and Robert Kirkpatrick.
     New York. Noonday Press, 1957: 104–106.
(157) *What Is Literature?,* tr. Bernard Frechtman.
     New York. Philosophical Library, 1949.
(158) *The Words,* tr. Bernard Frechtman.
     New York. G. Braziller, 1964.

(159) SIST, ARTHUR J.
     "Non-Alienated Society: An Appraisal of Its Possibility in the
     Light of the Sartrean Problematic and of the Responses of the
     Pluralistic and Participatory Theories of Democracy."
     Ph.D. dissertation, Yale University, 1971.

(160) SMELSER, NEIL.
     Essays in Sociological Explanation.
     Englewood Cliffs. Prentice-Hall, 1968: 49.

STRAUSS, LEO.
(161) "An Epilogue."
     In Storing, Herbert J., ed.
     Essays on the Scientific Study of Politics.
     New York. Holt, Rinehart and Winston, 1962: 327.
(162) *Natural Right and History.*
     Chicago. University of Chicago Press, 1953: 202–251.
(163) *On Tyranny.*
     New York. Free Press of Glencoe, 1963.
(164) *What Is Political Philosophy? And Other Studies.*
     Glencoe. Free Press of Glencoe, 1959.
(165) Page 14.
(166) Unsigned. "New Philosophers: Criticism of Marxism by French
     Philosophers." *Time* 110 (September 12, 1977): 29–30.

(167) TRUMAN, DAVID B.
     The Governmental Process: Political Interests and Public Opinion.
     New York. Alfred A. Knopf, 1951.
(168) Pages 8–10.

(169) TUCKER, ROBERT.
     The Marxian Revolutionary Idea.
     New York. W. W. Norton, 1969: 37–53.

WALZER, MICHAEL.
(170) *Just and Unjust Wars: A Moral Argument with Historical Illustra-*
     tions.
     New York. Basic Books, 1977.
(171) *Obligations: Essays on Disobedience, War, and Citizenship.*
     Cambridge. Harvard University Press, 1970.

Notes

(172) WELDON, T. D.
The Vocabulary of Politics.
Harmondsworth. Penguin Books, 1953.

(173) Pages 61–62.

(174) WILD, JOHN.
Plato's Modern Enemies and the Theory of Natural Law.
Chicago. University of Chicago Press, 1953.

(175) WINCH, PETER.
The Idea of a Social Science and Its Relation to Philosophy.
London. Routledge & Kegan Paul, 1958.

(176) WOLFF, ROBERT PAUL.
Understanding Rawls.
Princeton. Princeton University Press, 1977.

(177) WOLIN, SHELDON S.
Politics and Vision.
Boston. Little, Brown & Co., 1960.

(178) WOOD, ALLEN.
"The Marxian Critique of Justice."
Philosophy & Public Affairs 1, 3 (spring 1972): 244–282.

(179) WOODWARD, K. L.
"You're Entitled."
Newsweek 85 (March 31, 1975): 81.

Index